CLOSING THE GAP

5 steps to creating
an Inclusive Culture

Teresa Boughey

Praise

'This is a rare example of a book that truly spans engaging storytelling with hugely informative and practical guides. *Closing the Gap* is littered with reference points, insightful research examples and numerous weblinks. If you think that creating an inclusive organisational culture is a huge undertaking, you're right, but *Closing the Gap* is an excellent resource to assist in starting your journey or evaluating your progress. In her writing Teresa has inspired me to "rise up", to be challenged to stand on the shoulders of those before me and I will certainly use TRIBE5 to reach out and support those who will, hopefully in turn, go beyond my watermarks too. I know my version of *Closing the Gap* already looks more like a workbook well-thumbed with pages and vast sections highlighted and tabulated with sticky notes.'

— Stuart Branch
Group People & IT Director, Weetabix

'One of the things I worry about as an Inclusion and Diversity professional is whether there is something I am not doing that I should be. Teresa's wonderful book, in its easy-to-read conversational style, not only reassured me that I am doing a lot of the right things, but also guided me to several impactful approaches, tools and resources that I had overlooked. With insights from her personal experience and backed up with a variety of case study examples, TRIBE is not only comprehensive and insightful, but also practical and supportive, explaining the key concepts then taking you step-by-step through how to implement these best practices. Each section also has a handy checklist so you don't miss anything! I would highly recommend *Closing the Gap – 5 Steps to Creating an Inclusive Culture* to others who are looking to get an overview of the scope of the work that needs to be done, and how to do it.'

— Brian Ballantyne
Senior Programme Manager:
Inclusion & Diversity, Amazon
Author of *Confessions of a Working Father*

'Creating an inclusive culture has never been more important for businesses. Factors such as the changing workforce, attracting new clients, differentiating your brand and engaging with employees present leaders with significant challenges. Building a diverse and inclusive organisation – whether large or small – is a business imperative and should be on the top of the agenda. Teresa Boughey's *Closing the Gap* is a helpful guide using practical real-life examples and providing a framework for leaders and boards.'

— Gary Kildare
Chief HR Officer, IBM Europe

'Belonging is fast becoming the D&I solution of the future and to achieve this we need to ensure our efforts in this space are delivered in the right way. *Closing the Gap* is an excellent book for anyone starting off on their D&I journey and even for the seasoned D&I professionals. Teresa has captured key Diversity, Inclusion and Belonging principles within the book and provided some real, workable examples of how to put these into practice. The tribe5 model is a great tool to use to further the D&I agenda in any organisation and I would definitely recommend the book to everyone who really wants to make a difference in this space.'

— Asif Sadiq MBE
Diversity, Inclusion and Belonging thought-leader

'As an inclusion and diversity professional, I'm often looking for new ways to assist me in explaining the importance and methods of creating an inclusive workplace culture, but in a way that makes sense to others. It's here where Teresa Boughey's *Closing the Gap – 5 Steps to Creating an Inclusive Culture* really triumphs. By creating the TRIBE5 methodology, she has demystified what can be seen by some as the "abstract concept" of inclusion and diversity with a clear, step-by-step and immensely practical guide to achieving an inclusive workplace culture where diversity would naturally thrive. This book is full of useful case studies and practical advice which will help anyone starting their journey to creating an inclusive workplace culture, as well as being able to provide new ways of working for inclusion and diversity practitioners from across any industry.'

— **Barry Boffy**
Head of Inclusion & Diversity,
British Transport Police
2018 Winner Inclusive Companies Award:
Diversity Champion (Public Sector)

'*Closing the Gap* is an indispensable guide for all HR professionals and managers with any desire to further their diversity and inclusion goals. The current fundamental shift within organisations toward building positive working communities that contribute to wider society makes this book particularly apt for 2019. Diversity and inclusion are hugely beneficial to business, not just from this perspective but to attract and retain staff and customers and build an effective workforce, which can only help growing businesses. In this book Teresa helps businesses shape their future of work with her 5 steps to creating an inclusive culture.'

— **Emma Burrows**
Partner, Trowers & Hamlins LLP

'Diversity and Inclusion is a hot topic. Lots of businesses are saying "we are committed to Diversity and Inclusion", however many struggle with taking action. *Closing the Gap* is the book that organisations need to help turn their commitment into action. Teresa addresses key areas such as how to make the recruitment process more inclusive in plain English, so no more excuses for not recruiting a diversity workforce.'

— **Vivienne Aiyela**
Senior Diversity and Inclusion Consultant,
The People Engine

'Whilst the phrase "Diversity is what you have – Inclusivity is what you do with it" is oft repeated within organisational life, the fact of the matter is that there is still a lot of work and minds that have to be changed in order to address issues such as inequality in gender pay, exclusion though age or disability or biases confirmed through selection and assessment to find the "faces that fit". The amount of information placed here by Teresa will allow those in positions to influence to make changes is to her credit. It's clear, easily digested and provides numerous tools. What we need now is for organisational leaders to pick this up, critically review their environments and ask – "How can we do better?"'

— **Mark Stringer MSc AFHEA MABP MCIPD**
Lecturer and Director of OPHRM International
Programme Department of Organizational
Psychology, Birkbeck College, London

RETHINK PRESS

First published in Great Britain in 2019 by Rethink Press
(www.rethinkpress.com)

Contents

To my husband whose boundless support, love and kindness I treasure (but sometimes forget to say). And to my mum – everything I am, you helped me to be. You'll be forever in my heart.

Preface

I've written this book for managers, senior leaders, board directors and CEOs who just don't know where to start when it comes to creating an inclusive workplace culture that embraces diversity.

The words 'diversity', 'inclusion' and 'belonging' may strike fear, dread and confusion into some individuals as much as they offer hope, desire and possibilities for others. But in truth, our human desire to be in an environment in which we feel safe and respected by others is not a new concept. The need to feel included, for our effort to be rewarded and recognised, and to be provided with training and opportunities for new challenges is nothing new either.

Abraham Maslow, Humanist Psychologist, first introduced his motivation theory in the early 1940s, and his five-tier Hierarchy of Needs is one of the best-known theories of motivation. In accordance with Maslow's model, we often refer to the psychological and safety levels required for human existence as our basic needs. At a foundation level Maslow describes the basic human needs as air, water, food and sleep.

Maslow argued in his theory that while people aim to meet basic needs, they also have a desire to aim higher, in order to ultimately achieve self-actualisation. The second tier of Maslow's model is the physiological need for security of employment, health and property. The next tier moves into human social needs: love, family, friends, connecting with others, building communities and creating a sense of belonging. The fourth tier is self-esteem: the need to feel accomplishment, to be rewarded and recognised for effort; the need to be a unique individual respected by others, who feels confident of their achievements and respects the unique differences of others.

Finally, Maslow argued in his theory that people aim to achieve self-actualisation, which is when an individual realises their full potential within an environment. Self-actualisation includes a lack of prejudice.

Why am I reminding you of this – because Maslow's theory is certainly not new? Well, it's because boards up and down the country appear to struggle with the legislation and the social demand placed upon them when it comes to creating work environments where all employees feel safe, respected and truly valued for their unique differences.

I've heard business leaders question what diversity and inclusion really mean. I've heard them asking *why* they need to embrace and engage with diversity and inclusivity at all. And, I've heard their questions in relation to what they need to do and concerns about not knowing exactly where to start.

For many, closing the gap and creating an inclusive workplace culture feels like an enormous issue to address. It either continues to sit in the 'too difficult' pile, or business leaders undertake piecemeal initiatives – neither of which creates impetus, and the gap fails to close.

Closing the gap is not simply a 'them versus us' initiative that pits race, gender, age, disability, religion or belief, and sexual orientation against each other. Instead, it is recognising that businesses are all about people – people who come together to a place they call 'work'. A place where diversity and inclusivity foster a sense of belonging; where contributions, unique differences and talents are valued with parity.

Implementing successful diversity and inclusivity policies as part of any business's standard practice shouldn't, therefore, be viewed as a tick-box exercise to satisfy government regulations. The positive impacts far outweigh paying lip service to its requirements. In closing the gaps that undeniably exist (on a large scale) in UK plc, businesses will discover the exponential value in retaining individuals who exit the workplace to grow their families or care for loved ones.

Recognising that millennials are demanding a different working environment opens up new ways to recruit the right talent for organisations but it also presents challenges for organisations as they need to consider and adapt their operating practices, which includes flexible working and environments where employees are highly engaged and where performance is rewarded, rather than presenteeism.

An inclusive environment creates more opportunities to gain competitive advantage and brand recognition, particularly when the whole employee base feels valued, respected and equally rewarded.

I know only too well, having operated at board level for many years, the challenges that leaders face every day. Making decisions that enable an organisation to compete in the forever changing economic landscape; decisions which often include mergers, moves, upscaling, downsizing, restructures and new product launches, all with the intention of business survival, growth and success. In other words, decisions which ultimately impact on its workforce. Time and time again, I've sat in board meetings where senior leaders discuss and debate business agenda items. At best, people are the last agenda items to be discussed; at worst, they're completely overlooked.

My corporate experience has taught me that, although many organisations purport to regard people as their most important assets, more often than not the words and the music just don't align, people generally being the first casualties during difficult economic times. Recruitment activities result in a replication of the existing workforce demographic. Women who take time away from the workplace for maternity leave at best return to a lesser role, having made a request for flexible working, and at worst don't return at all (I know, as I was one of them). Senior leaders meet requests to work at home with mistrust and scepticism. They give promotions readily to those who 'fit', and those who don't are encouraged to exit. Remuneration would be geared towards rewarding the delivery of targets, regardless of the behaviours used to get there. And so, the erosion of the workplace culture continues.

Throughout my corporate journey, I have seen and experienced inclusive opportunities first hand where organisations have embraced diversity positively, reaping the rewards of improved employee engagement, increased productivity and enhanced profitability. I will share some of these stories in this book.

I've also experienced occasions where, tragically, organisations have got it wrong and discriminated against employees. The impact and reach of this is wide ranging, from damage to employee engagement, brand, and company reputation, to damage to the organisation's bottom line as it faces legal fees and fines imposed through employment tribunal claims.

The more aware and in tune an organisation is with its people and the incredible differences they bring into the workplace every day, the more successful it will be. And it is inclusion and diversity that hold the key to this success.

My business acumen and passion for diversity and inclusion have seen me awarded one of fifty UK Female Entrepreneur Ambassador Awards, as well as a seat on the All-Party Parliamentary Group for Women and Enterprise and the Women and Work All-Party Parliamentary Group. I'm privileged to have the ability to influence the UK government about the support individuals require as they embark upon various stages of their entrepreneurial journeys, but I'm also passionate about the need for organisations to accelerate their commitment to diversity and inclusion, and to widen the scope to include all underrepresented groups.

If you've not already started on this journey, then there's never been a better time than now. It's vital that organisations provide the right environment for everybody to feel able to be the best version of themselves. I promise you, it will pay dividends.

Creating an inclusive organisation and closing any diversity gap isn't going to be a quick fix because change won't happen overnight. It requires the unpicking of deep-rooted traditions, which have often been embedded into organisations for generations. It requires a shift in mindset and behaviours, as well as a review of operational practices. To make a real and sustainable difference, everyone – board directors, their leadership teams and the entire workforce – needs to adopt a holistic approach to diversity and inclusion. One which recognises, values and utilises the individual differences and talents of all employees.

I've written this book to provide you with a clear framework so that you have a path to follow on your diversity and inclusivity journey. It's time to move it off the 'too difficult' pile. You can read the book cover to cover; alternatively, you can dip into each chapter and focus on specific areas. Whichever route you take, my tribe5 Diversity & Inclusion methodology will enable you to take stock of your own organisation and shape your action plan to close the diversity gap and create a workplace culture that is truly inclusive.

If you follow the tribe5 Diversity & Inclusion methodology, you'll set the drumbeat for generations to come.

Introduction

The status quo

Diversity and inclusion in the workplace go far beyond quotas and data submission. In the UK, the government introduced, following business consultation, a requirement for those organisations with more than 250 employees to submit gender pay data on an annual basis. This business-led initiative was aimed at addressing pay disparities between female and male employees with a commitment to closing the gap within a generation. Diversity and inclusion shouldn't be viewed as a fad. It's not the latest business initiative. It's not a tick-box exercise, nor is it quota filling. And it won't go away. Race, age, disability, religious belief, sex and sexual orientation are important business topics that urgently need highlighting.

Diversity and inclusion matter not only to our current workforce, but they are also going to be essential for future generations. Millennials and their successors are already demanding different ways of working and organisations will need to respond to this. Technology advancements will bring welcome opportunities for inclusion, enabling organisations to deliver increased business performance results and solutions to customers outside of traditional working hours within an office environment, thus reducing operating costs as well as retaining valued employees who may otherwise exit the workplace. Organisations need to stem the loss of talent due to the personal life choices which many employees face. Our aging population also has a significant contribution to make to economic success. They too require a different way of working – one that focuses on customer experience and performance as opposed to presenteeism.

Diversity sits at the heart of these challenges. The key for any business leader is knowing how to adopt a sustainable, holistic approach to weaving diversity throughout the organisation.

Reporting on gender-based pay has provided many organisations with the opportunity to take the first steps in addressing disparities. For some, the figures have (finally) exposed the elephant in the room, the data clearly identifying an imbalance in female representation which has been neglected for generations. While the data may have uncovered an uncomfortable truth for many organisations, failure to take positive action to address the imbalance will result in an even more ugly truth year on year.

It's vital that UK plc as a whole takes the necessary steps to understand what differentiates 'gender pay' from 'equal pay' and how important it is to recognise an individual's unique differences and, in some instances, their 'protected characteristics'. It enhances awareness about what these are and why they exist, and aids understanding of the legislation that regulates them. What do we mean when we say diversity, inclusion and intersectionality? Each one of these represents a minefield to business leaders who often don't have the necessary information, or the right tools, to navigate their respective paths.

Research into gender diversity continues to highlight the overwhelming need for, and the benefits associated with, a more diverse workforce. Global Management Consultants McKinsey make it increasingly clear through their research that companies with more diverse workforces perform better financially.[1] The research suggests that when companies commit themselves to diverse leadership, they are consequently more successful in:

− Attracting top talent

− Improving their customer reputation

− Increasing employee satisfaction

− Aiding decision making, which in turn leads to increased profitability returns, thus achieving a diversity dividend

Since 2010, the UK government has endeavoured to shine a spotlight on the issue of gender disparity within UK companies. Lord Davies of Abersoch (then UK Minister of State for Trade, Investment and Small Business) was commissioned in 2010 to conduct an independent review, primarily within FTSE 100 companies, into the under-representation of women at board level. His findings resulted in an initial voluntary target being set to increase the representation of

---

1 'Why Diversity Matters': Vivian Hunt, Dennis Layton and Sara Prince, McKinsey.com (2015) and 'Delivering through Diversity': Vivian Hunt, Lareina Yee, Sara Prince and Sundiatu Dixon-Fyle, January 2018

women in FTSE 100 boards to at least 25 per cent. This target was successfully achieved by October 2015, albeit mainly through the increased appointments of female non-executive directors. The figures clearly demonstrate that what gets measured gets managed and change occurs.

This business-led initiative on closing the gap on gender disparity continued to remain in the spotlight through the work of Sir Philip Hampton and the late Dame Helen Alexander. Their November 2016 report set out recommendations which widened the scope further across UK companies, making it the most ambitious voluntary initiative to close the gender gap. Targets for 2020 included:

– FTSE 100 and FTSE 250 companies should aim to achieve a minimum of 33 per cent female representation across Executive Committee and their direct reports

– FTSE 350 companies should also aim to achieve a minimum of 33 per cent female representation on their boards

The November 2018 Hampton-Alexander Review considered FTSE 100 companies to be 'on track' to achieving the 33 per cent target if they continued progress at the current rate.[2] While progress had been made across FTSE 250 and FTSE 350 companies, the Hampton-Alexander review highlighted that a step change would be required in order to reach the targets set.

The UK remains one of the few countries where the government has resisted the need to impose formal quotas on achieving gender balance in favour of a voluntary business-led approach, albeit the annual reporting of gender pay making it somewhat less optional. This has attracted praise from other countries that observe and commend the approach and the progress, albeit slow, which is being made.

What has become apparent is that shining a spotlight on the important topic of the gender pay gap is bringing significant results. However, there's still more to be done to create truly inclusive companies. Organisations must reflect the communities within which they operate. While it's important that organisations continue to close the gender gap, they must also remove barriers for all underrepresented groups. One area leading to greater transparency is the mandatory publishing of ethnicity pay information. Some larger organisations have taken the initiative and have voluntarily shared their data, however this is not a practice adopted by all. The UK government closed its Consultation on

---

2   Hampton-Alexander Review 'FTSE Women Leaders: Improving Gender Bin FTSE Leadership', November 2018, https://www.gov.uk/government/publications/ftse-women-leaders-hampton-alexander-review

Ethnicity Pay Reporting in January 2019.The outcome of the consultation is likely to require large companies to report ethnicity pay information using a prescribed methodology, on a mandatory basis. This staunch and consistent approach will enable the benchmarking of ethnicity reporting to take place and for progress to be measured.[3]

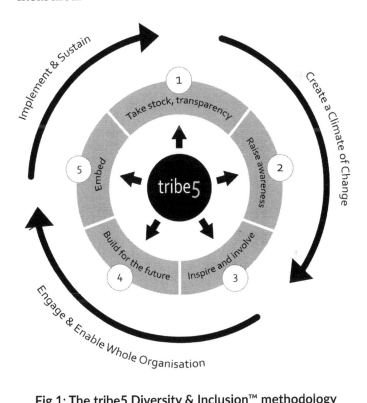

Fig 1: The tribe5 Diversity & Inclusion™ methodology

---

3   https://assets.publishing.service.gov.uk/government/uploads/
     system/uploads/attachment_data/file/747546/ethnicity-pay-
     reporting-consultation.pdf

Throughout this book, I will show you how to follow my tribe5 Diversity & Inclusion methodology. This model can be used at any point in your organisation's progress towards creating an inclusive workplace culture, providing you with a clear framework.

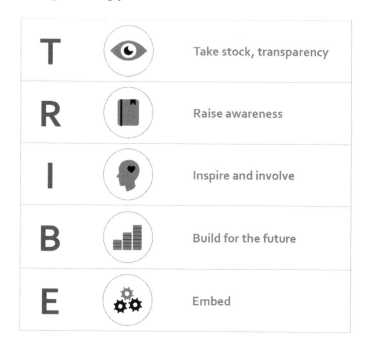

T	Take stock, transparency
R	Raise awareness
I	Inspire and involve
B	Build for the future
E	Embed

T – Take stock, Transparency. The first step is to establish the 'as is' position. In other words, the truth of your current diversity and inclusion position. It's imperative that you know what this is as it gives you a starting point.

R – Raise awareness. Weaving diversity and inclusion throughout an organisation is not the role of one or two individuals, but something which involves everyone. It enables your organisation to be representative of your marketplace, customers and the community of which you are part.

I – Inspire and Involve. Role models and ambassadors are vitally important, as is having mentoring programmes that inspire and involve everyone. Reinforcing and celebrating behaviours that are inclusive infuses diversity within your organisation.

B – Build the future. This requires a change to organisational behaviour to identify the right talent and ensure that structures and working practices reflect your organisation of tomorrow.

E – Embed. Resilience will be imperative, as will zero tolerance. Bringing about any change, particularly change that involves a new way of thinking and being, is never going to be an easy journey and will take time. It's important to check in regularly with what's working and what's not. But the ultimate aim is to reach a position where diversity and inclusion are firmly embedded into your organisation's culture, no matter who is at the helm.

Throughout this book, I will guide you through each of the five TRIBE stages, demonstrating that inclusiveness and diversity have a real and valid contribution to make to the success of your organisation. Given the high returns that an inclusive culture can bring, it's better to start upon this journey now than be left behind.

Resources and tools

The five steps set out in this book are powerful. I know from my extensive experience they will enable you to build a sustainable diversity and inclusiveness strategy. To assist you further, I've created a number of resources and tools. These include the diversity and inclusion scorecard, which is freely available for your organisation to take, whatever its size. It will enable you to measure your organisation against the five key stages you require to build an inclusive workplace culture. This simple yet effective business tool will offer you an instant insight into how much you have achieved already, or where you have gaps that need attention, providing recommendations for enhancements in these key areas. Regardless of your position in your inclusion journey, I would encourage you to take the scorecard – it's free and there's always room for improvement.

To find out more about the scorecard, go to: www.junglediversity.com/diconsultancy/tribe5-diversity-inclusion/diversity-inclusion-scorecard/

A diversity and inclusiveness strategy is nothing without implementation. But implementation can be hard to achieve alone, so I would recommend you look at joining an accelerator programme, such as the ones offered by my business, Jungle – because it's a corporate jungle out there. These programmes enable you to be part of a high-performance community dedicated to one thing: creating an inclusive organisation culture which is built on excellence.

Hopefully by now you'll be getting a sense of just how passionate I am about the importance of building an inclusive workplace culture and the benefits it brings. I'm therefore delighted you're reading this book; I'm thrilled you've chosen to join me in accelerating your diversity and inclusion journey.

Hold on tight and let's get started!

SECTION 1

TAKE STOCK AND TRANSPARENCY

Take Stock – Introduction

I have introduced you to the tribe5 Diversity & Inclusion methodology and explained how, through its implementation, your organisation will be able to create an inclusive culture and build a diverse workforce. Now it's time to explore the first part of the tribe5 Diversity & Inclusion methodology, which is all about **taking stock** and **transparency**.

When you start to bring about any sort of change, it's really important that you understand your current 'as is' position. To do this, you have to stop and take stock.

Best practice would be for organisations of all shapes and sizes to take stock of their entire workforce on a regular basis. As an absolute minimum, this should occur annually, but the more frequently that it reviews people data, the more in tune an organisation is likely to be with the people who work within it. Remember, measurability is important: *what gets measured, gets managed.*

Taking stock is essential in establishing where you are so that you can gain clarity on the actions to take to move towards where you need to be. But being transparent with your data discoveries is of equal importance. Don't shy away from what the data is telling you, even if it represents an uncomfortable truth. Use your people data proactively – be honest, build a plan, and communicate this plan widely so that everyone feels part of the inclusive company you're setting out to create.

During this section, I will:

- Tell you what people data is important to gather

- Help you to identify where you need to start

- Give you hints and tips to help you take stock and cascade with transparency

The 'Take Stock' chapters will support anyone who may have fallen down on reviewing and reporting on people data so far. They will help those who are worried by the current or emerging legislation. They will also act as a useful reminder to a seasoned leader, who may wish to leave a copy of this book (with this page bookmarked) on the desk of someone who is unclear on where to start when it comes to building an inclusive company. The tools, techniques, hints and tips will help everyone to understand not only the why, but also the how.

Establishing the 'as is' position

The 'as is' position is the truth in relation to the current diversity within an organisation. Establishing this is critical since it will give clarity on the starting point. However, gaining an overview of people data can often be easier said than done.

I understand only too well the challenge of trying to obtain accurate employee data, having previously been responsible for gathering and reporting on people. Getting to the bottom of the people data was challenging to say the least! HR held some information (often on spreadsheets). Payroll also held employee information, and more often than not, the two sets of data didn't align. A further frustration was that the technology platforms didn't talk to each other. All of this tended to lead to inaccurate data being generated and reported upon.

The General Data Protection Regulations (GDPR), which came into effect in May 2018, have strengthened and modernised laws to further protect the handling, processing and retention of personal information. Many organisations will therefore have taken appropriate measures to ensure ongoing GDPR compliance, and as such will likely have streamlined the way they hold and process employee data. But the questions remain – what is the best people data to gather to enable you to take stock of your company's inclusion position, and where can you find it?

There are several sources from which you can take stock of your people data, and in these next chapters I will guide you through some of them. The areas I highlight are by no means the only places to explore as there's always new information available, whether it be through internal company data or external resources such as reports, research, white papers and publications. The key thing is to be conscious of your current data, continually looking for ways to improve, and then implementing the changes.

Begin with the end in mind

– Taking stock is a vital first step. This gives you a snapshot of time, albeit a historic snapshot. It's therefore important when taking stock to look forward. In the words of the late business guru Stephen Covey, from his acclaimed book *The 7 Habits of Highly Effective People*, 'begin with the end in mind'. This approach enables you to reverse engineer your diversity and inclusion strategy plan.

Take a moment to consider the following questions:

- What does it look and feel like to work in your organisation now?

- What's working well?

- Where are you heading as an organisation?

- What will it feel like to work within your organisation when you have developed an inclusive culture?

- What will the benefits be to your employees, your customers, your shareholders and your business performance when it's achieved?

- How will you know you have achieved it? What will you see, feel and hear?

Reverse engineering your desired outcome is a highly successful approach. Here's a case study so you can see for yourself.

CASE STUDY - BEGIN WITH THE END IN MIND

When a Group HR and IT Director joined a fast-moving consumer goods (FMCG) organisation, the first thing he had to do was listen. He wanted to really get to know the business and take stock of the current culture. What was working well? What was the strategic direction of the business, and what needed to change to deliver against the strategic objectives?

He knew from previous experience what good looked like. Equally he recognised that he couldn't replicate what he had done before – it needed to look and feel appropriate for this organisation. The Director was respectful of the culture that had been formed within the organisation and the pedigree that had grown because of it.

From the information he obtained during his first 100 days, he shaped a people strategy. A key focus area was the creation and implementation of an employee engagement and reward strategy, for which the company has received industry recognition via national awards. Then came the focus on talent strategy. What was the company going to do to attract talent going forward?

It completed a mock gender pay reporting exercise ahead of the government's submission deadline to fully understand the data, check for errors and take focused action to close the gap. The company then communicated this information transparently with the workforce, so employees understood why the gap existed and what steps the company was taking to address this. The results of this inclusive people strategy have increased the numbers of women in leadership roles within the organisation.

This company was one of the first large companies to submit gender pay data. While the company does still have a gap, it also has a strong plan in place to continue to make the gap smaller.

Facing up to reality

Taking stock requires you to face up to reality so that you can fully understand what you need to overcome. Looking at the 'hard data', which we will explore in more detail over the next few chapters, is one element, but you will also have to explore the 'softer' side of your organisation – the hearts and minds, the limiting beliefs, the biases (unconscious or otherwise) and the desire to change. These softer elements can in fact be the hardest aspect to manage, influence and change, but understanding and facing these obstacles is essential as you move towards a more inclusive and diverse culture.

Horizon scanning

Finally, look externally to see what outside factors are likely to help or hinder you as you travel along your journey to create an inclusive culture.

As part of the Look Back, Look Forward and Plan approach, it's important to consider what's happening on the horizon. Use business tools such as PESTLE (Political, Economic, Social, Technological, Legal and Environmental)[4] to conduct an analysis through the lens of creating an inclusive culture. This is a great

---

4   Created in 1967 by Harvard professor, Francis Aguilar.

way to explore the external environment and consider how it will affect your organisation.

Creating an inclusive workplace culture is an enabler for organisations, not a burden or barrier. With that in mind, let's get started.

Take Stock – Resourcing

Attracting top talent to any organisation is vital for gaining a competitive advantage.

This chapter explores some of the recruitment practices an organisation can adopt to broaden the diversity of its workforce. It's important to highlight that there's no 'one size fits all' and what works for one organisation may not be appropriate for another. However, the practices which I'm sharing in this chapter have been implemented across a wide range of organisations and industry sectors, and have had a positive impact on closing the gap and building a more inclusive workplace culture.

So, where to start?

Recruitment strategy

Creating or conducting a thorough review of your organisation's recruitment strategy is a good first step.

 When doing so, give consideration to the following:

- What are your company recruitment goals?

- What recruitment methods do you currently use and for which level (in-house, external recruitment partners, agencies, advertisements, online, job fairs, refer a friend, head-hunters)?

- How and where are jobs advertised?

- What is the language and tone of your job adverts?

- Are the roles and responsibilities clear for those involved in the recruitment process?

- What selection assessment criteria do you use?

- What is the process you follow for advertising vacancies internally? When and how do you do this?

- What employability checks do you carry out?

- What is your company's approach to paying expenses to interview candidates?

- How do you on-board successful candidates?

- What criteria do you use to measure recruitment effectiveness?

- How does your recruitment strategy link to the overall business strategy?

- What other company policies does your recruitment strategy link into, eg retention, reward and talent development?

By considering these questions, you can start to reflect upon your organisation's current recruitment practices. Look at the effectiveness of your approach to understand how you can create an innovative recruitment practice, ensuring that you're attracting and selecting candidates swiftly, consistently and from the widest possible pool.

Job architecture

Prior to any recruitment, review your organisational requirements; don't just replace like for like. Start by taking a look at current team structures and talent plans to ensure that any internal candidates have a fair and transparent opportunity for career advancement. This also offers a great opportunity for you to review the job role itself. It might currently be full time, but perhaps it could be part-time, or filled by flexible working or a job share. By broadening the scope of the role, you're likely to make it more widely accessible.

Job descriptions

Review each role description regularly to ensure that it reflects the new requirements of the job. Your focus should be on the competencies of a job, as opposed to specific tasks that an individual would be required to undertake. It's also important when you're reviewing job roles and job descriptions to ensure the tone and language contained within them are unbiased.

Working with external recruitment partners

Getting to know, understand and trust your recruitment partner is great for building a long-term relationship. Often external recruitment partners have worked with organisations for years and have essentially become an extension of the organisation. However, it's important to revisit those relationships from time to time to ensure that your recruitment partners fully understand the company's strategic direction, your recruitment strategy, and importantly, your approach to diversity and inclusion. Your external recruitment partner will generally be the first contact that any potential employee has with your organisation. It's essential that they represent you in the right way.

But best practice recruitment methods are only one part of the story. It's important that you find out your recruitment partner's approach to diversity and inclusion and ask relevant questions. Who's handling your account? What experience do they have of diversity and inclusion? How does their approach to diversity and inclusion show in the advertisements they produce? What solutions do they present to you about broadening the candidate search? Are they signed up to the Recruitment & Employment Confederation code of practice? This code includes principles on diverse recruitment as well as setting standards for ethical business practice. Further details can be found at https://www.rec.uk.com/membership/compliance/code-of-practice2/test. It's your recruitment partner's responsibility to showcase how they will support your organisation in drawing talent from the widest possible pool.

In 2018, the Women and Work All-Party Parliamentary Group put out a call for the submission of evidence regarding the approach to recruiting women in the twenty-first century. One approach, shared by external recruitment companies and in-house recruitment teams, was the practice of blind CVs, ie removing any information that could suggest an individual's race, gender, age or other such characteristic, as well as removing reference to the educational institution which they may have attended. Another recommendation was to ensure that the shortlists of qualified candidates include more than one woman. A *Harvard Business Review* article concluded that the chances of women being selected for senior leadership roles were not improved if only one female candidate made the shortlist.[5]

Choose the words and pictures carefully

When looking at running recruitment adverts, you should consider any copy which agencies propose. Words such as 'high-energy' and 'driven' could imply that candidates would need to be able-bodied and young; driven could also have masculine connotations. It's also important to consider the imagery that is used when advertising job vacancies.

Show me the money

As part of the recruitment process, you should clearly communicate at the outset the salary range you're offering for the role. Having this information available at the outset enables the applicant to know what they can reasonably expect. It also ensures transparency for both internal and external candidates. If salary for the role is negotiable, then state this clearly at the commencement of the recruitment process.

---

5   Johnson, S.K., Hekman, D.R., and Chan, E.T. (2016). If there's only one woman in your candidate pool, there's statistically no chance she'll be hired. *Harvard Business Review*, 26(04).

Methods for selection

Make sure your recruitment strategy sets out the methods you'll use for candidate assessment. Are skills-based assessments appropriate and relevant to the job you're offering? If they are, it's important to ensure that you have taken measures to enable accessibility for all parties.

It's not unusual for organisations to host assessment centres or selection days. These can, and often do, include an element of physical activity. While on the surface they may seem fun and engaging, you really do need to consider the relevance of such activities. Are they required to fulfil the job? Will the candidate be undertaking similar tasks as part of their day-to-day job role if they are successful? Is the task or activity inclusive? Will it enable you to select the right candidate for the job role? If you cannot objectively justify the activity you have in mind, then think of another activity to assess the candidates' suitability.

Technology

How can you use technology as part of your recruitment strategy? Will technology enable or limit candidate sifting? These considerations form part of the recruitment strategy you implement within your organisation.

Interview structure

Detail the approach you will take to the interview itself in your recruitment strategy. Interviews are typically conducted by line managers, and occasionally an HR professional may be part of the panel. But managers often rely upon limited training on how to carry out interviews, and then spend many years picking up bad habits.

I would advocate that anyone involved in making selection decisions (including external recruitment partners) must be fully trained in effective recruitment practices. They should understand the role that they play within the recruitment process, how they are brand ambassadors for the organisation, and be fully up-skilled in terms of recognising the biases that they may hold, which may affect their decision-making abilities.

Some organisations use interview panels when making appointments. It's important to ensure that these interview panels are balanced, which can include having representation from across minority groups. If you have no female and/or minority representation at senior level, consider involving others within the organisation to enable broad and balanced decisions to be made.

Some organisations prefer to conduct 'informal' interviews. This approach can make candidates feel at ease quickly and encourage a free flow of conversation, but it's important to recognise that this is more likely to allow unfair bias to creep in and influence any decisions.

Structured interviews, particularly when they're linked to a competency-based framework, provide a level playing field for candidates' assessments. They ensure that candidates are all asked the same questions using a structured and pre-determined format. A clear scoring and grading system throughout the selection criteria enables the candidate assessments to be comparable, reducing any potential for and/or impact of unconscious bias.

Internal recruitment strategy

When you're developing a recruitment strategy, ensure that you consider the approach you wish to adopt for internal recruitment. Think about implementing a clear and transparent career path for all job roles within your organisation. These career paths should be widely available to all employees and regularly updated so every employee can understand what they require to move to another role or level within the organisation. This will enable them to make informed career choices.

CASE STUDY – CAREER PATH

A leading manufacturing organisation conducted a review of its workforce and identified a pattern which had developed. Many of its engineers plateaued in terms of career advancement when they reached a certain level. Very few had put themselves forward for promotion, and the majority of senior hires were external candidates.

The organisation wanted to understand the reasons for this. It trained its managers to hold career conversations with team members, and conducted a series of focus groups.

These two initiatives uncovered the following: There was a general lack of understanding about other roles within the organisation

- Employees felt that they did not understand the skills and competency required to undertake different roles
- They didn't feel able to talk about wanting to explore other job roles for fear it would impact on their current role
- Some technical experts believed career advancement meant 'people management responsibilities', which they either didn't want or didn't have experience of
- The internal recruitment system was ineffective – some said they hadn't known a role was available until an external appointment had been made

This information led the company to overhaul its internal recruitment system and make the process of applying for any role across the organisation more transparent. Job roles were grouped into families, and the company created clear and simple career paths for each job family. Career path roadshows took place across the organisation so that everyone understood what the roles were, why the company had done this and what it meant for them. Every employee received a copy of the career path guides, and they were also made available on the company intranet.

To embed the career paths framework further, the organisation changed the format of its regular performance reviews to include career conversations. In addition, it made clear connections with the career path framework within its learning resource centre (a previously underutilised resource). Employees were able to access books, online courses, leadership training, as well as coaching and mentoring programmes.

By setting out the roles available in this way, the organisation ensured that those who worked for it were able to see all of the internal jobs. Employees could understand what was required for them to move to other roles, knowing the skills and competency for each. This transparent approach put the employee clearly in the driving seat when it came to making their own informed career choices.

An internal recruitment application system enables internal candidates to understand the process they need to follow when applying for other roles within an organisation. The process should be fair and consistently applied. I've seen it work well in some companies, especially when the process includes internal stakeholder and/or line manager sponsorship for internal applications. This allows transparent conversations to take place between the employee and the line manager. Or if the relationship between the candidate and line manager feels challenged or the candidate feels unsupported by their manager (sadly, this does occur), the employee can seek sponsorship from elsewhere in the business.

An approach such as this enables organisations to have transparent and honest conversations with employees about their desired career choices. These career conversations should form part of regular performance conversations. We will cover this in more detail in *Build For The Future – Training And Development*.

Candidate feedback

The feedback candidates, including internal candidates, receive when they are unsuccessful should be an integral part of the recruitment process. This feedback needs to be comprehensive and supported. Internal candidates being given a development plan and, where possible, mentoring to enable them to not only understand their gaps, but also explore how these gaps can be closed. Whenever an employee puts themselves forward for an internal promotion, make sure this triggers a review of where they appear within the mechanism your organisation has in place to capture and develop talent.

It's important to set out in your strategy the level of feedback that will be available to unsuccessful external candidates. Make this a point for discussion with your recruitment partner (if you work with one). If candidates feel that they have been discriminated against during the selection process, especially if they can prove that the discrimination was in relation to a protected characteristic such as gender, age, race or sexual orientation, then they could potentially bring a claim against your organisation. It's therefore imperative that all candidates are treated fairly.

I remember when I worked many years ago for a holiday company. It was the company's approach to treat every candidate who applied to work for it as a potential customer. The organisation firmly believed that if a candidate had a bad experience with it, regardless of whether they were successful in securing the job for which they applied, they were unlikely to book a holiday with the company in the future. If, however, they were unsuccessful, but had a great candidate experience, they would still wish to travel on holiday with the company. I'd encourage you to adopt this approach.

Searching far and wide

Talent is all around us, but if we only look in the same places, then the supply becomes limited. Research shows that there is a rich pool of 'returners' – talented individuals, a high proportion of whom are women, who have taken extended career breaks, often to raise families. They have a wealth of skills and experience to offer an organisation, but may require support to rebuild confidence or upskill any technology gaps.

There are a number of external schemes in operation which provide these individuals with such support. Take time to connect with those schemes. Understand the work they are doing. Learn how you might get involved either by supporting a programme, running your own programme, or offering placements to/hiring returnships.

We will explore returnships further in the *Build For The Future* section.

Vetting and employability checks

There are clear guidelines set out by the UK government in relation to the checks an employer must make on job applicants. These include right to work in the UK and criminal checks.

Any check you make should be appropriate for the job role for which the candidate is applying. Inappropriate use or the mishandling of employment checks can potentially lead to legal challenges.

You can find further information at www.gov.uk/employers-checks-job-applicants

When taking up references you should also consider asking for references in relation to experience gained outside of the workplace such as any voluntary work, or membership of groups or clubs. This provides an opportunity for those who may have employment gaps to showcase the skills and experience gained from outside the work environment.

It's important to note that while an employer is likely to undertake relevant checks on a job applicant, the applicant is also likely to do their own checks on a potential employer. This might include exploring the organisation's annual report and accounts, or online social media platform. If your company meets the criteria for the now annual submission of gender pay data, then employees may look at this data. This will give them a good indication of the culture of your organisation and your approach to diversity and inclusion.

Recruitment monitoring

All recruitment practices must be measured, monitored and recorded. This enables your organisation to clearly track successful recruitment approaches.

 Here are a few things you can consider:

- Number of candidates applying

- Candidate demographics (if available)

- Selection criteria used

- Who was involved in the selection process

- Time taken to fill the vacancy

- Source of candidate attraction

- What were the candidate rejection stages – who left the process, when and why

- Internal applicants vs external candidates

- Make-up of selection panels

- Training undertaken by hiring managers

It's important to track the candidate retention period, with a retention objective being a good target to set your external recruitment partner. It's all well and good sourcing candidates, but if the talent doesn't stay, you need to understand why. Making a poor recruitment decision can be costly to your organisation – it can disrupt your workforce, it can impact on business performance, and it can be expensive to have to commence the hiring process again. Equally, it can be a costly career choice for the individual concerned.

Resourcing summary

Having the right talent and resources available within your organisation is critical. It's therefore important to do it properly, and right! If you get it wrong, you'll have an unhappy workforce. It'll not only be costly to continue to hire individuals but you're also likely to exhaust the potential source of talented candidates. Your brand reputation could become damaged, and worst case, you could face employment tribunals.

When you do it right, you'll build your brand and your reputation. You'll have employees within your organisation who bring a richness of skill, talent and expertise through their unique differences. Employee engagement will increase, productivity within your organisation will improve and business performance will grow.

Take Stock – Reward And Remuneration

As we learned in the Preface, Maslow's hierarchy of need sets out the stages of motivation. The foundation of Maslow's model focuses on our physiological needs: air, food, water and sleep. The next stage is the need for safety: the desire to find a job, earn sufficient money to be able to provide shelter, and a safe and healthy lifestyle. It's therefore no wonder that the salary employees are paid is such an intrinsic component of the psychological contract between an employee and an employer at the commencement of employment.

Fig 2: Maslow's Hierarchy of Needs

Let's face it, for the majority of employees, the salary that they earn through working for a company is often their only means of generating an income. This income should enable them to meet at least their basic levels of needs, as defined by Maslow's hierarchy.

When a company's reward strategy is well constructed and implemented, employees will feel motivated and engaged. They're likely to feel their efforts are being recognised and rewarded appropriately. However, when they sense imbalance and unfairness, employees can become dissatisfied. Their resentment builds, their morale becomes low and their performance dramatically reduces. Your brand reputation may be damaged as employees choose to leave your organisation or take legal action to redress the balance. Ensuring that all those who carry out work for your company are fairly and appropriately rewarded is therefore vitally important. Having an inclusive reward strategy that is competitive, fair and offered equally to all employees will enable you to attract and retain top talent, build your brand reputation and attract new clients.

The scope of your reward strategy

The scope of your reward strategy should not only extend to those who are directly employed on a full- and part-time basis, but consideration should also be given to third parties such as contractors, associates and temporary workers. Many procurement/tender processes now focus not only on value for money and delivery of service, but will also scrutinise a company's approach to the pay it gives to contractors and third-party associates who are often relied upon to deliver such contracts. For those organisations operating under UK employment legislation, one way to demonstrate such a commitment is by going further than the minimum wage set out by the UK government and pay all employees the real Living Wage.

In 2018, there were over 4,700 companies accredited as Living Wage employers.

'The Living Wage Foundation report that 93% of those companies who have signed up to their Living Wage Charter and become accredited have seen enhanced business benefits. 86% say it has improved the reputation of the business, 75% say it has increased motivation and retention rates for employees, 64% say it has differentiated themselves from others in their industry and 58% of employers reported that it's improved relations between managers and their staff.'[6]

To become a Living Wage accredited employer, you need to pay the real living wage to all directly employed staff, and have a plan in place to pay contractors a living wage too. Further information about the criteria and application process can be found at www.livingwage.org.uk

Taking stock of your reward and remuneration

Taking stock of your reward and remuneration not only enables you to manage budgets and forecasts, but provides clarity on whether the pay and benefits you are offering are competitive. But where do you start and how do you know if your reward strategy is fair and inclusive? It can be a minefield, but there are many specialist companies that can help build and shape a reward strategy with/for you. In this section, I will highlight some of the steps you can take, even

---

6   www.livingwage.org.uk

if you are unable to invest in the support offered by reward consultants and companies.

Analyse your data

Gather all of the data together on your employees and their pay. Ideally, this data should be segregated so that it can be analysed. If you have a pay grading system, then ensure that you also report on the pay grades/bands to gain further clarity on the various pay grades/bands/job families offered within your organisation.

This is an opportunity to reflect upon how widely understood the pay grades are within your organisation. Do employees fully understand the clear pathway that's available to them to enable them to move and progress within pay grade structures or are they shrouded in secrecy?

External benchmarking

Have your pay grade structures and salary bands had any form of external benchmarking? Externally benchmarking the salaries offered within your organisation enables you to understand how competitive you are in the marketplace.

Many recruitment companies offer free online salary checking tools, allowing you to benchmark your salary against market rate by simply searching job title and location. Remember that employees and potential employees are likely to use these tools too.

Employee benefits

You should also take stock of the benefits offered to employees, including all monetary and non-monetary benefits. It should include any benefits offered through salary sacrifice schemes such as childcare vouchers, bikes to work or healthcare cashback schemes.

Does your organisation offer flexibility in terms of unpaid leave, sabbaticals or statutory or enhanced provisions for maternity, paternity and adoption leave?

Some organisations only allow access to benefits at the point of appointment, after which they are no longer available. These benefits are typically healthcare and/or pension related.

 These are just a few examples. Take a moment to consider the following:

– What non-monetary benefits do you offer?

– What monetary benefits do you offer?

– Are these benefits open to all employees, regardless of length of service and/or job level/grade?

- When are they offered? Are they only offered to employees upon commencement of employment, or are employees reminded of the benefits available to them each and every year?

- How well are these benefits promoted to employees?

Here's a case study to show the components that can make up a rich reward strategy.

CASE STUDY – ANNUAL AWARD STATEMENT

A manufacturing company felt it important to be transparent with all of its employees about the rewards available to them. The intention of this activity was not only to showcase the rewards that were available, but also to remind employees that their reward for working for the organisation was wider than the basic pay they received and also included non-monetary rewards.

The organisation set about gathering employee data and listed all of the benefits that employees were eligible to participate in. These included benefits which had both a monetary and non-monetary value. The company wanted to showcase these benefits to employees each year, so it decided to provide every employee with an annual reward statement that detailed:

- The basic pay the employee received
- Whether they had received any overtime
- Their participation in the company's holiday buy-sell scheme
- Whether they were part of a flexible working arrangement
- Any pension contributions
- Any membership of a share-save scheme
- Their holiday entitlement
- A reminder of the pay grade to which they belonged
- Membership of the gym services which the company subsidised
- A reminder of the onsite catering facilities, which the company subsidised
- Details of eligibility for maternity, paternity, or shared parental leave

All of this information was detailed in one single document, which was sent to every employee on an annual basis. This level of transparency reminded employees of the vast array of benefits on offer, allowing them to see that their reward within the organisation was greater than the pay packet that they received every month.

Equally, the exercise of compiling this data provided the organisation with an opportunity to take stock of the benefits it was offering to its employees. It helped the board to understand who was taking up which benefits, whether they needed further advertisement to encourage increased participation, or whether the board needed to explore alternative reward benefits to meet employees' modern-day needs.

Not only did the organisation provide these reward statements to employees, it also made the topic of reward an item on the employee forum agenda. This gave the employee forum an opportunity to reach out to employees and obtain their views on the rewards and benefits offered within the business, coming up with alternative suggestions where necessary.

Pay and grading systems

Another area to consider is whether you operate pay grades/bands within your organisation. Some organisations seek professional advice from external companies that offer support with the design and implementation of a pay reward and grading system. Others may be governed by historic pay and grading structures and annual union negotiations. And some organisations continue to operate without clarity on their pay bands and structures at all. While it may give an organisation freedom and flexibility to pay whatever it wants to secure the talent it desires, it provides a complex and potentially illegal situation for those already working within an organisation or to those looking to join.

Whichever route you decide to follow, it's important to ensure that your pay and grading system is fair and consistently applied. Failure to do so may leave your employees dissatisfied, as well as potentially exposing your company to claims on the grounds of equal pay.

Having a transparent grading structure, which is linked to initiatives such as career paths, provides a clear framework for employees who wish to progress professionally within the organisation, and enhance their earning capability as a consequence.

Salary negotiations

Salary is often negotiated at the commencement of an employment relationship. From a gender perspective, research suggests that men are more likely to negotiate a higher salary rate at the time of appointment, often endeavouring to negotiate sometimes beyond the recognised market rate, while women tend to be more conservative.

CASE STUDY – SALARY NEGOTIATIONS

A leading fast-moving consumer goods (FMCG) manufacturing organisation was seeking to make a leadership appointment. The role was advertised externally and the final selection was whittled down to two candidates – one male, one female.

The job advertisement had indicated a salary range, thereby setting candidates' expectations. However, during the interview process, salary discussions took place. The male candidate boldly stated his desired salary. He felt his skills, experience and expertise merited the upper end of the salary scale on offer. But the female candidate, when asked the same question, stated what her current salary was rather than entering into a negotiation for an increase.

The company decided to offer the position to the female executive, awarding her the salary she mentioned. But the HR Director argued fiercely on her behalf that her salary should match what the company had been prepared to pay the male candidate. They also pointed out that paying the lower salary would leave her earning less than her counterparts/colleagues on the leadership team. The HR Director maintained the company should pay the salary suitable for the role and consistent with others in the same role, regardless of the candidate's stated expectations. This view prevailed, and the female candidate was appointed with the higher salary, matching both the advertised role and her colleagues.

In a *Personnel Today* article, Women's Trust chief executive Carole Easton said:

'We have to break the cycle that traps women in low pay. Women often start work on a lower salary than men, move to a new job and are paid based on their previous wage, as opposed to what they or the role are worth – so they continue to be paid less.'[7]

Open dialogue – don't silence salary conversations

Many contracts of employment and company policies contain clauses which prevent employees speaking about their salaries. This traditional approach often stems from a fear factor, a belief that having explicit clauses in contracts of employment which silence salary conversations means that employees won't be tempted to talk with each other and find out what their colleagues are paid. In truth, this doesn't work.

Notwithstanding the GDPR around the sharing of personal data, combined with an individual's personal desire not to discuss how much they earn, employees *do* discuss salaries.

When there is a lack of transparent published salary information on job adverts and grading systems, employees look to fill in the gaps themselves and speculate. Gossip becomes rife, especially when it's pay review or bonus award time, or when someone

---

7   Jo Faragher, 22 Aug 2018, 'Asking candidates about their current salary contributions to gender pay gap' www.personneltoday.com/hr/asking-candidates-about-current-salary-contributes-to-gender-pay-gap/

new joins the organisation. This in turn can have a negative effect on employee morale.

Transparent salary information on job adverts and grading systems makes it harder for companies to pay different amounts for similar jobs, regardless of gender, race, age or for any other reason.

Pay awards

There's already so much you need to consider in your reward strategy, but having a clear process for when and how you give pay rewards is equally important.

Some organisations are governed by formal union agreements. But if your organisation isn't, then you have an opportunity to ensure your process for reviewing and making pay rewards is fair and equitable. Involving additional stakeholders as well as employee forum members/employee representatives is a positive step towards making balanced and unbiased reward decisions.

Some companies choose to award standard percentage increases across the board on an annual basis. Others might have a salary pot which is distributed among those working in the department to which the pot relates. Some companies operate schemes whereby salary increases occur on the workers' employment anniversaries, and others award increases at set times of the year.

Pay rewards linked with performance are often used by organisations, although this approach can come under scrutiny because of biased decision making, particularly when there is a lack of balanced adjudication, structure and/or assessment criteria. The other thing to make sure of when you're offering performance-based pay rewards is to have a broad view of employee performance. Seek opinions widely, particularly as some managers may not have day-to-day interaction with their employees, or they may have formed biased opinions of individuals' performance. Consider performance on a behavioural basis in addition to task-based performance objectives. This last point is particularly important when you are looking to bring about change within a culture, which often starts with a change in behaviour.

There is no right or wrong approach to take (unless your approach is in breach of the Equality Act 2010). What is important is that you apply your approach fairly and consistently. It's also important that your process is transparent, widely known and understood by all the employees who work for your company.

Equal pay

There's still some confusion between equal pay and gender pay. Both are complex and have an overlapping relationship, but they are not the same thing, so I want to try to simplify this (as much as I can).

In simple terms:

- Equal Pay is legislation set out in the Equality Act 2010. It means that women and men performing equal work, of equal value for the same company must be paid equally.
- The Gender Pay Gap is the framework / mechanism. It is used to measure and report / publish the difference between men and women in the same organisation of average and median overall earnings.

Both equal pay and gender pay deal with disparity. The Equality and Human Rights Commission defines the difference between equal pay and gender pay as follows:

- Equal pay means that men and women in the same employment performing equal work must receive equal pay, as set out in the Equality Act 2010
- The gender pay gap is a measure of the difference between men's and women's average earnings across an organisation or the labour market[8]

---

8   www.equalityhumanrights.com / en / advice-and-guidance /
    what-difference-between-gender-pay-gap-and-equal-pay

Equal pay audit

Some organisations have also chosen to undertake an equal pay audit. This involves comparing the pay of men and women doing like or equivalent work of equal value in the organisation, and broadly has three main purposes:

- To identify any difference in pay between men and women doing equal work

- To investigate the causes of any differences in pay between men and women doing equal work

- To eliminate instances of unequal pay that cannot be justified

An equal pay audit is not just a data collecting exercise. It's an extensive process that requires companywide commitment, careful consideration and planning. The Equality and Human Rights Commission has set out five steps to conducting an equal pay audit:

Step 1: deciding the scope

Step 2: determining where men and women are doing equal work

Step 3: collecting pay data

Step 4: causes of gender pay differences

Step 5: developing an action plan

You can download further information as well as fact sheets from www.equalityhumanrights.com/en/multipage-guide/equal-pay-audit-larger-organisations

Gender pay gap reporting

As referenced earlier, the business-led and government-backed voluntary target for all FTSE 100 and FTSE 250 companies to ensure that at least a third of the people on their boards are women by 2020 is being monitored through the annual gender pay data reporting. These organisations will, as an absolute minimum, review the average and median overall pay for men and women once per year. The government has set out the data which employers are required to publish annually, the intention being to increase transparency around gender diversity and enable companies to focus their efforts on the steps they need to take to bring about necessary changes.

The six key reporting requirements are set out below:

Mean gender pay gap: The difference in hourly pay of male and female relevant employees	**Median bonus gender pay gap:** The bonus pay paid to female and male relevant employees
Median gender pay gap: The difference in hourly pay of female and male relevant employees	**Bonus proportion:** The proportion of female and male relevant employees receiving a bonus payment
Mean bonus gender pay gap: The bonus pay paid to female and male relevant employees	**Quartile pay bands:** The proportion of female and males in four pay bands: lower, lower middle, upper middle and upper quartile pay bands

This information can be found in greater detail on the CIPD website at www.cipd.co.uk/knowledge/fundamentals/relations/gender-pay-gap-reporting/guide

Other important points about UK gender pay reporting:

– Gender pay is not the same as equal pay

– Businesses and charities with more than 250 employees must publish their data by 4 April each year

– Public sector organisations must publish by 30 March each year

– Organisations must publish the data on their own website for at least three years, and must also publish the data on the Government website https://gender-pay-gap.service.gov.uk/

In addition to submitting gender pay data, organisations are expected to submit a written statement, on an annual basis, setting out the steps they intend to take to close the gap.

Ethnicity pay gap

While the spotlight has shone on the gap in pay relating to gender, research also shows a significant ethnicity pay gap. The UK government closed its consultation into the ethnicity pay gap in January 2019, and the response will inform future government policy on the approach which companies may be mandated to take in the reporting of ethnicity pay. In 2020 listed companies will be required annually to publish and justify pay differences between chief executives and their employees. What is clear is that more changes are on the horizon as legislation continues to emerge, you therefore need to widen the scope of your pay data analysis and be prepared for pay reporting to be rolled out in other areas in the future.

'Dodgy' data

The Equalities and Human Rights Commission (EHRC) has the important but lengthy task of scrutinising the gender pay data once submitted. *People Management* reported in an article that between 9 per cent and 17 per cent of gender pay gap data had potentially been submitted incorrectly by the 10,000 organisations with more than 250 employees.[9] In truth, I'm unsurprised by these figures. Many organisations are likely to have faced challenges in simply accessing, extracting and analysing their people data.

But this level of scrutiny clearly highlights there's no room for complacency. You can't just submit any old data in the hope that no-one notices. And the scrutiny doesn't end following the initial submission. The EHRC has written to the organisations it suspected of

---

9   Emily Burt, *People Management* 'Employers who supplied "dodgy" gender pay data face action by EHRC', 12 July 2018

misreporting on their data, requesting that they either correct or explain the data. While the most likely explanation for misreporting is a simple misunderstanding of the required calculations, failure to comply with the gender pay data requirements and deliberate misreporting come at a price. Organisations may become liable for legal action, as well as having to manage the negative publicity which could be generated among employees, customers and investors.

So, it's important to get it right. If you're still unsure about how you should be reporting your gender pay data, further information can be found on the UK government's website www.gov.uk/government/news/view-gender-pay-gap-information

Reward summary

Rewarding employees financially is an important ingredient for closing the gap and a major component of the psychological contract between an employee and the employer. Reviewing some of the themes we've covered in this chapter and creating a clear plan that sets out your company's approach to paying and rewarding your employees will help you to move closer towards building an inclusive workplace culture.

Take Stock – Company Policies And Procedure

Reviewing your company policies and procedures, checking that they remain compliant with relevant employment legislation and circulating them around the business to make sure managers are aware of any updates – these are tasks usually undertaken by the HR function. But this singular approach is insufficient when you're creating an inclusive workplace culture.

Of course, policies need to reflect the relevant employment legislation, but they also need to be easily understood and accessible to employees. In short, they need to be enablers as opposed to diktat set down by the company. However, more often than not, HR polices the policies. Managers, who don't understand the policies themselves, then lean on HR not only to translate them, but to do the people management for them.

Yes, policies should provide a framework that keeps an organisation operating on the right side of the law, but they should also enable a company to grow and prosper, helping employees to understand where they stand and to know what is expected of them. This in turn provides the framework which an organisation can use to address any conduct or behaviour which falls short.

The policies and formal practices in place within your company will say a lot about the importance you currently place on inclusion and diversity. Many of you will, I'm sure, review your policies regularly, but do they reflect the demands of modern-day life and do they enable you to create an inclusive workplace culture?

Let's take a look.

Respectful workplace

I'm certain that your organisation already has policies and procedures in place to deal with discrimination, bullying and harassment. Many organisations have seen an increase in the reporting of such cases following movements like Time's Up and #MeToo. The collective voice of these movements has seen women and men show strength in numbers, stepping forward to report cases relating to allegations of sexual harassment, bullying and unwanted behaviour in the workplace. Previously these individuals may have felt unable to voice their concerns, or in some instances they may have been silenced, unable to disclose past events.

If you've not already taken action to create a respectful workplace, then your organisation needs to do so now. You need to recognise the potential consequences of such negative allegations if they are not managed effectively. It's so important to have clear policies and procedures in place which set out expected workplace behaviour.

 Here are a few tips:

- Policies should be clearly written so that they are easily understood at all levels within an organisation.

- If you have employees whose first language is not English, consider translating your policies into other languages. Also, using a large font could be helpful for visually impaired employees.

- Your employees must have easy access to these policies. They shouldn't be hidden away (in a folder on a shelf or in someone's drawer) and employees shouldn't have to go through their line manager or HR in order to access them.

- Your policies should set out the importance of treating others with dignity and respect.

- You should have a clear procedure for handling complaints so that those making the complaint can be confident they will be taken seriously. This also serves as a stark reminder to the perpetrator that there will be consequences for any unacceptable behaviour.

- Managers should receive training on policies, enabling them to act quickly and fairly in the event that a complaint is made.

- All complaints and allegations should be closely monitored.

There are many policies which your company can review and implement when you're creating an inclusive culture. Let's take a look at a few.

Agency workers and contractors. Many companies use agency workers and contractors for projects, to meet an increase in workload or fill skill gaps. The rights of agency workers have increased therefore it's important that you have policies and procedures in place to ensure that your treatment of these workers is not less favourable then permanent employees. For further information see www.gov.uk/agency-workers-your-rights/your-rights-as-a-temporary-agency-worker

Customers. It may not be necessary to have policies in place on how to treat customers fairly, but a good organisation knows the importance of treating customers with courtesy and respect, otherwise you'll never get any repeat business. However, when building an inclusive culture it's important to recognise and meet the needs of customers from different backgrounds. Ask yourself if there's any more you could do to make your services or products accessible to all.

From the language you use to making your premises or website compliant with disability recommendations, look at every stage of the customer journey and take stock. Make your customer journey experience easy and understandable. This applies equally to customer interaction over the telephone, via email or in a customer facing environment.

Family-friendly policies. Have a set of policies in place which make it possible for employees with children to thrive in the workplace as well as satisfy their private lives. These policies can include maternity, paternity or adoption leave, parental leave, or time off for dependants, to name but a few.

When you're implementing your family-friendly policies, carefully consider the requirements of modern-day families, particularly as many statutory family-friendly schemes no longer meet their needs. Shared parental leave pay schemes, for instance, are less generous than those offered under enhanced maternity pay.[10]

---

10 www.peoplemanagement.co.uk/experts/legal/
why-you-should-have-family-friendly-policies

Gender reassignment

The Equality Act of 2010 makes it unlawful to discriminate against someone or treat them unfairly because of gender reassignment. Having a clear gender reassignment policy in place will enable your employees to feel safe and supported.

Megan Key, Equality Manager for the National Probation Service and trans activist, talked openly at an Inclusive Companies event about her journey to change her gender while working for her employer. Megan shared that one of the reasons she felt comfortable, safe and confident to do this was because there was a proactive and positive gender reassignment policy in place within her organisation. Hers is just one example of how policies are there to support employees and to enable them to be the best that they can be.

Disciplinary policies and procedures

Sometimes it's necessary to invoke a formal procedure when an employee's conduct or performance falls below the expected standards. The focus, however, should be on improvement, not punishment. And, of course, your disciplinary policy and procedures should be clearly set out and widely accessible.

As a qualified mediator, I understand only too well the importance of independent dispute resolution. Mediation is a form of alternative dispute resolution (ADR) and can be a productive and cost-effective way to help parties reach an agreement.

If a company's disciplinary policy has been exhausted, then an employee may, subject to meeting the relevant criteria, bring a claim through an employment tribunal. Handling disciplinary matters needs to be done with care and respect. It's important to make sure your policies are clearly written and applied with fairness and equity so that they do not disadvantage or negatively impact any particular groups of employees.

For UK businesses, I recommend that your disciplinary procedure follows the Advisory, Conciliation and Arbitration Service (ACAS) code. You can find further information at www.acas.org.uk/index. aspx?articleid=2174

Grievances

Let's face it – disputes and disagreements happen. We're all individuals with our own unique views and opinions, and unfortunately, we can't get along with everyone all of the time. Sometimes colleagues fall out, or best intentions can be misinterpreted, causing a misunderstanding. Having a procedure in place which everyone understands and can follow is a great way to nip disagreements in the bud quickly.

When concerns or disagreements are unable to be resolved informally it's important to have in place a robust procedure which ensures that everyone feels listened to and supported to resolve any issues objectively.

Flexible working

Flexible working is a key component for creating an inclusive workplace culture. Rather than viewing flexible working requests as an individual's desire to seek alternative arrangements to your organisation's current norm, focus on what the business stands to gain by using flexible working to enhance performance and attract talent.

Your flexible working policy should define the provisions you offer, clearly setting out how you deal with flexible working requests. Flexible working isn't just something which working parents desire. Many millennials want to have the ability to work flexibly, as do those who are approaching retirement but wish to continue working after they reach pensionable age.

At a time where work-life balance is really valued, having an inclusive flexible working policy in place will help you to attract and retain the best talent and be seen as an employer of choice.

Health and wellbeing policies

Keeping employees safe at work is not just good practice, it's a legal requirement. I'm sure you'll have all the normal safety at work guidance and risk assessments in place already, but I'd encourage you to look further at your policies. For example, is your dress code policy restrictive or discriminatory? Do you make suitable provision for religious dress or articles of faith?

A healthy workforce is a happy workforce and leads to reduced absence due to sickness, higher employee engagement and improved business performance. Having clearly defined policies on health and wellbeing will help your employees to understand how they will be supported in the event of sickness absence. Such policies need to be inclusive and not discriminatory.

Consider the procedures your organisation has in place to support your policies, checking that these are understood by the line managers who have to implement them. Repeated absences impact the operational performance of an organisation, so it's important to get to the root cause.

Formulaic systems for measuring absenteeism have been around since the early 1980s. While they may offer a system to calculate the impact of absence, they fail to understand the human element associated with health and wellbeing. Carefully research whatever system you choose to ensure that it matches your values and approach to the health and wellbeing of your workforce. It should be fully understood by all employees and applied consistently.

When looking at your health and wellbeing policies, it's also important to consider the approach you want to take to support employees returning to work after a period of absence. This may involve working with healthcare professionals as well as the application of your flexible working policy.

Switching from a mindset of 'sickness absence' and focusing on 'health and wellbeing' is a subtle but important change which will help you set the tone for your inclusive culture.

Pay and reward policies

You might want to consider conducting an equal pay audit at the start of your diversity and inclusion journey. I explored this in more detail in the previous chapter and highlighted the benefits while cautioning that it's not a task to enter into lightly.

Any policies, including reward policies such as bonuses and performance-related salary increases, should be based on objective criteria and easily understood by leaders and employees.

Managing peak performance

Operating at peak performance is the key to the success of any organisation. However, managing employee performance can at times be challenging. Some employees require little direction and have the drive and determination to succeed, whereas others require much more management time to steer them in the right direction.

The implementation of a performance management procedure can help employees clearly understand their role and contribution to the attainment of company targets and objectives. It also provides a clear framework for managers to follow to ensure that they manage and support their employees fairly and consistently.

A performance management procedure shouldn't be punitive; it should be an objective and transparent process. Employees should be encouraged to set their own stretch targets (with the aim of achieving the overall company goal) and feel empowered to track their performance. It's important that they receive recognition when they are on track or exceeding their expectation, and also feel able to ask for help and guidance when necessary.

One of the tools I use when working with clients to create a high-performance culture is the **Action Plan for Success.** It's not a performance improvement plan; rather, it's about focusing on what the employees need to do to succeed in their roles. The employee completes the document themselves, thus taking responsibility for their actions and creating greater ownership.

I recommend all your employees have an Action Plan for Success, even your highest performer, as everyone can raise the bar. Feel free to download a copy at www.junglehr.com/free-resources

Procurement

Many procurement/tender processes now focus not only on value for money and delivery of service, but will also scrutinise a company's approach to the pay it gives to contractors and third-party associates. You may want to consider reviewing your own approach to how you reward the contractors who provide services to your organisation, but consider your response if you were asked to provide this level of information as part of a tender process.

Reasonable adjustments

Reasonable adjustments are important for job applicants, employees and customers. They ensure that working life and access to products and services are free from avoidable disadvantages. There are many things which companies can do to make reasonable adjustments.

 These might include recruitment and promotion policies and procedures which will have a huge influence on your current and future workforce. This is a reminder to look at every stage of your recruitment process, from advertising to interviews, and consider how you communicate with prospective employees and former employers. Your recruitment procedures must be transparent and accessible to all applicants (internally and externally). Job descriptions need to focus on objective criteria relating only to the position advertised.

Consider if your procedures and the language used could impact negatively on particular protected characteristics.

If you already have groups which are underrepresented within your workplace, think carefully about putting in place strategies to change this.

Training and development

When it comes to diversity, inclusion, equality and treating people fairly, ask yourself if you have regular training in place for managers and staff so that they know how to conduct themselves and how to support and be supported in the workplace?

Work-related training that can lead to an individual's growth and development should be accessible to all, and should also take into account the needs of minority groups. It's therefore important to have in place policies and procedures which help provide clarity for everyone around these important areas.

Whistleblowing

The Public Interest Disclosure Act 1998 is the key piece of UK legislation which protects individuals who want to report workplace wrongdoing. 'Whistleblowing' is the term used when a person feels unable to raise their concerns about information or activity that is deemed illegal or unethical directly with their organisation or a prescribed body. Instead, they report the alleged wrongdoing to an external body in the belief that they are doing so in the public interest. Individuals blowing the whistle may seek protection under the legislation if they can show that their allegation was made in the public interest as well as in their own reasonable belief.

Anyone making allegations of sexual harassment is likely to qualify for protection as claims often reference an unlawful or potentially criminal act. The question which remains, however, is whether such a disclosure would fall within the public interest. To be clear, I'm not answering this question in this book but I wanted to highlight this important point. Movements such as Time's Up and #MeToo have shone a light on behaviour in the workplace, particularly that which is far from respectful. You need to be prepared to deal with these issues sensitively and appropriately because how you do so sets the cultural tone of your organisation.

Employment legislation is complex – it's therefore best to seek legal advice.

Take stock – Company policies and procedures summary

It's great to have a set of well-formulated policies covering all your people, but make sure they don't sit on a shelf in somebody's office. Bring your policies to life.

Make sure they are well written and easy to understand and let your employees know how to access them and keep them updated. After all, policies should be enablers not barriers to the creation of an inclusive workplace culture.

Take Stock – Leavers

Leaver information is often overlooked, but it's an important barometer for your organisation's culture. It's important to establish why people are leaving your business, particularly as hiring, developing and retaining your workforce is a huge investment. Analysing your leaver information is also an important component when it comes to formulating your diversity and inclusion strategy as it will enable you to gain clarity on the real reasons why people leave your business.

Where to start

Tracking your leaver information via your payroll and/or HR system will give you quantitative data, ie the number of leavers, from which department, when they leave and how long they've worked for the company.

 This information is helpful in assisting you to analyse things such as:

- The characteristics of who is leaving the company (if you hold this information)

- What job role they occupy at the time of leaving

- How long have they worked for the company?

- How many roles have they held while working for the company?

- Did their career develop while they worked for your company or did they remain in a particular job role?

- Details of their benefits package

- Did they take up all benefits which were available to them?

- Did they take all their holiday entitlement?

- Which manager(s) did they work for/report to?

- The reason for leaving

All of the above information will help you to formulate a clearer picture of any trends or patterns which are arising.

The real reason for leaving

One of the most difficult things to establish firmly is an employee's 'real' reason for leaving your organisation. A popular way to obtain this information is through exit questionnaires. Typically they are offered to employees on their last day, or even after they have left the organisation. These are often paper-based questionnaires, inviting a series of 'yes/no' answers, possibly with a small text box for the individual to offer any additional comments they wish to make. Notwithstanding vexatious employees who have lots to say, many employees feel reluctant to complete an exit questionnaire honestly.

Another way in which organisations gather qualitative leaver information is through exit interviews. In my experience, unless these have been set up well, they are often ineffective. Typically, at the point at which they are conducted, the leaver has already checked out of the organisation mentally and emotionally. They may feel inhibited, unable to be honest in their feedback. It's not unheard of for employees to report feeling reluctant to state their real reasons for leaving for fear of reprisals by way of poor references for future job roles.

When an organisation creates a culture that is inclusive, employees feel more able to speak honestly about their career aspirations. They are then likely to share any frustrations they have within the workplace during their employment tenure rather than at the point of exit.

Performance and career conversations

Performance and career conversations with individuals should take place on a regular basis with all employees. In many organisations however, this doesn't always happen. At best a manager might have an occasional quick 'one-to-one' meeting with an employee where they rattle through the tasks which need completing, at worst a year's worth of feedback is shared with the employee during their mandatory 'annual appraisal'.

In addition to talking regularly to employees about their performance I would recommend that separate, but regular career conversations take place. These discussions should focus purely on the employee and should include exploring an individual's career aspirations and not deviate onto 'task' topics.

Effective career conversations enable managers to better understand employees, professionally and personally. The dialogue needs to be totally open and needs to provide a balance where managers take the time to show a genuine interest in the professional skills, career path and work-life balance their employees desire, at the same time as being transparent with employees about what the organisation is or isn't able to offer. These open and healthy discussions enable the organisation to understand the talent within their organisation and employees to know where and how they can move forward in their careers.

In some instances, these conversations can reenergise an employee and give them a fresh focus and/or career opportunity. If the environment is supportive of career and performance discussions, it comes as no surprise when an employee does decide to leave the organisation. They do so with dignity, preserving the reputation and brand of the organisation and you're more likely to learn the true reason for their departure as opposed to a superficial version.

Tracking leaver information

Tracking leaver information will permit you to gain clarity on any patterns.

 Take a moment to consider the following:

- Are employees leaving from a certain department? Does this highlight concerns with regards to management capability which need to be addressed through leadership development?

- Is there a lack of career opportunities, which is resulting in talent departing your organisation to utilise their talent elsewhere?

– Are individuals not returning from maternity or paternity leave? Do you have initiatives in place such as flexible working and maternity, paternity and adoption provisions which reflect modern family life and enable you to retain talent from the widest and most diverse workforce pool?

– Do you track leaver information against any employee relations matters such as bullying or harassment grievances / complaints? This will provide an opportunity for you to understand any inappropriate behavioural patterns and address them within your business.

Creating an inclusive environment where employees have multiple routes to share leaver information is vital. It will give you an alternative perspective into your organisation's culture and will help you to drill down into the real reasons why people leave. There are, of course, individuals who, despite everything you do, will leave your organisation feeling vexatious. But in the main, when they're presented with a safe, inclusive and supportive environment, departing employees will feel that they've been given the opportunity to be listened to and understood.

Take stock – Leaver summary

Leaver information is a rich source of information. It's certainly something that I would encourage you to weave into your people data dashboard and report on monthly at your board meetings, setting targets against it for improvement. Make sure your employees feel part of a safe and inclusive environment while they work for you, and in the main you will be rewarded by rich and honest information when they leave. Drilling down to the real reasons why people are leaving your organisation will give you clarity on any negative patterns that are emerging, allowing you to address them with training where necessary.

Take Stock – The Importance Of Transparency

Having conducted a diagnostic review of your data the next step is to acknowledge the findings.

The *Taking Stock* section may have exposed some surprises and possibly even identified some inherent subconscious bias in your organisation.

As uncomfortable as the findings may feel, it's important to own them and acknowledge your organisation's current cultural position. It's not about basking in glory or pointing the finger of culpability. It simply means taking a leadership role and acknowledging that in some instances (to quote Marshall Goldsmith), 'What got you here won't get you there'. It's about acknowledging that you don't want to risk alienating a potential consumer, and you don't want to risk alienating employees either as they could choose to take their expertise and ideas to your competitors. The world has changed and will keep changing, so it's time for your organisation to change, culturally and socially. Not because regulation says so, but because times have moved on.

An enabler, not an excuse

Some organisations will use the data they uncover as an excuse. The BBC reported in its article 'Top 10 Worst Excuses for Not Appointing Women Executives', some of the excuses that consultants heard when undertaking interviews with senior executives as part of the Hampton-Alexander Review.[11] The appalling excuses included 'All the "good" women have already been snapped up' and 'Most women don't want the hassle or pressure of sitting on a board'. While progress is being made in closing the gap, it's sad to hear that these beliefs still exist.

It's going to take time to unpick deep-seated beliefs and break with traditions. When you're faced with generations of ingrained behaviours and beliefs, though, you must start somewhere, and communicating transparently with your workforce is a great place to start.

---

11   www.bbc.co.uk/news/business-44310225

Communicate with transparency

I provide details on how you can communicate with clarity in 'Build For The Future – The Role Of Communication'.

 However, here are a few ways in which you might wish to share your data:

–   Present the 'Take Stock' information to your board / leadership team in the first instance.

–   Be honest, open and transparent with the picture that the data is painting

–   Create briefing cascade documents so that each member of the leadership team can consistently communicate the findings of your diversity and inclusion diagnostic review to their team.

–   Extend the cascade process to become a two-way process, ie cascade the information, but build in a mechanism which allows for a period of reflection. Then have a vehicle in place which enables all employees to comment on the information and offer suggestions for improvement.

–   Consider the tone and language you use in any communication – is it jargon free? Is it easy to understand?

–   Create a people data dashboard and report on this monthly so that you can hold the leadership team to account, track progress, make changes when progress is slow and celebrate when change happens.

– Share the information with employee forums. Where your organisation has not yet established these, you might want to consider creating a similar employee group.

– Assist the forum members to digest the information. Provide them with a framework to enable them to reflect upon the findings, communicate with the workforce, and feed their recommendations for change back.

Cascading gender pay data

There are organisations which are now required to gather gender pay data and publish it on the government portal, as well as displaying it on their company website on an annual basis. This approach forces organisations to become more transparent with their data. However, research compiled by YouGov reported that 44% of workers at organisations with 250 or more employees say their employer has still not made the gender pay gap clear to them.[12] This point was evidenced when I was having a discussion with one of my clients. Here's their case study.

---

12 YouGov.co.uk – 'Gender pay gap still not clear to four in ten employees despite reporting legislation'

CASE STUDY – A MISSED OPPORTUNITY

During a leadership development programme, one group of delegates was invited to reflect upon a time when their company had shared and communicated business information well to the workforce. Another group was invited to reflect upon a time when their company didn't communicate effectively. Both groups were also asked to consider the impact of the communication and the implications it had for the workforce, coming up with some ways in which the information could have been shared differently.

The group that was invited to reflect upon a time when the company communicated poorly cited the reporting of its gender pay position to its workforce. The strength of feeling within the group could really be felt as the delegates verbalised their frustrations. They reported that the methods of communication the company had used had been one way, skimming over the data leaving those on the receiving end of the communication with more questions than answers.

The group also expressed concern around not understanding the difference between the gender pay gap and equal pay. A big missing piece for them was why and how the gap had arisen and they had no understanding of the company's plan to address this. As a consequence, the intended communication cascade failed. The managers who were expected to share the information with the workforce felt ill equipped to do so. They felt unable to answer any questions, so it was easier to simply pin the communication to the noticeboard, hoping that those who wanted to see it would.

These leaders were truly disappointed by this missed opportunity – an opportunity for an organisation to acknowledge and own its diversity and inclusion status. That's not to say that the organisation isn't taking the data seriously or putting in measures to close the gap. It just highlights that in the absence of transparent and effective communication, employees can be left with unanswered questions that are often filled with rumour or speculation and a continuation of a 'traditional norm'.

Gathering the data is one step, but it's what you do with that data which truly counts. Sharing this information widely with your workforce and raising awareness about the importance of creating an inclusive workplace culture is the next transformational step to take to effect change and close any gaps.

Take stock – The importance of transparency summary

We've discussed in detail how to take stock of your 'as is' position regarding diversity and inclusion, but the sad fact remains that some companies are still not being transparent about the data they gather as a result. It's essential that your organisation owns its true position and takes transparent action to fill any gaps. Such action must be understood by everyone involved in making the change. In other words, ensure no employee is left with unanswered questions. Equip your line managers with the tools, skills and information they require to cascade all findings down throughout the organisation, answering each and every question the employees may have. Without this transparency, your taking stock will be a missed opportunity to close the gap.

Take Stock – Summary And Checklist

Taking stock is essential in establishing where you are so that you can gain clarity on the actions you need to take in order to move towards where you need to be. By now, I hope you feel clearer on where to start when it comes to taking stock and where to find important data to give your employees insight into your current culture and working practices.

Being transparent with your data discoveries is of equal importance. Don't shy away from what the data is telling you, even if it represents an uncomfortable truth. Use your people data proactively to build a plan, which we will cover in 'Build For The Future – Talent Planning'. Then communicate this plan widely to your workforce so that everyone feels part of the inclusive company you're setting out to create.

An inclusive workplace culture, where everyone feels valued and respected for their unique differences, is not something which occurs overnight. Your starting point may be very different from that of another person reading this book. Regardless of where your starting point is, though, it's important to review, adapt and change regularly so that you continue to improve.

Let's recap on how you can take stock and cascade with transparency.

Take stock checklist

— **Resourcing**

☐ Do you have a strategy in place which sets out the methods you use to attract and select the best talent from the widest possible pool?

☐ Do you monitor the recruitment process to identify the stage of the process at which candidates are dropping out?

☐ Do you take the opportunity to review job roles and structures whenever a vacancy arises?

☐ Do you have a process in place for internal applications, including feedback and development support?

☐ Do you train all the individuals involved in the selection process so that they fully understand their role, including any biases they may hold when making selection decisions?

- **Retention**

  ☐ Do you have an appraisal and performance management process in place?

  ☐ Is the appraisal and performance management process two-way?

  ☐ Is the process widely understood and inclusive?

  ☐ Are all managers fully trained to hold performance conversations confidently and effectively?

  ☐ Are employees able to speak openly about their personal career aspirations?

  ☐ Is the process linked with other people strategies such as talent planning or reward?

- **Reward and remuneration**

  ☐ Do you have a reward strategy that is fair and inclusive?

  ☐ Do you have pay grades/bands which are widely understood by all employees?

  ☐ Do you have a fair and equitable process in place for reviewing and making pay awards?

  ☐ What does your pay data tell you?

- **Health and wellbeing**

  ☐ Do you have policies in place which support employees during illness?

  ☐ Is the environment conducive to a stress-free workplace and a good work-life balance?

  ☐ Does your company offer care benefits and social events to bond teams?

- **Policies and procedures**

  ☐ Are your policies and procedures enablers or barriers to diversity and inclusion?

  ☐ Do you offer flexible working – ie the opportunity for part-time or home working, flexible hours, parental leave and paid overtime?

  ☐ Do your family-friendly policies reflect the requirements of modern-day families?

  ☐ Have you woven inclusion and diversity into your procurement policies?

  ☐ Do you train all your managers on your policies and procedures?

- **Leavers**

  ☐ What does your data tell you in terms of your turnover?

  ☐ Do you carry out exit interviews to understand the 'real' reasons why people leave?

☐ Do you track leaver information to establish any underlying patterns?

– **Transparency**

☐ Do you share information with your employees in an open and transparent way?

☐ Is the information jargon free and easy to understand?

☐ Do you own the findings of your people data or do you hide the information away, preferring to keep this 'confidential'?

Now you have come to the end of your journey into taking stock of the 'as is' position and making sure your findings are transparent and easily understood by everyone in the organisation, let's move on to the second stage of the tribe5 Diversity & Inclusion methodology: Raise Awareness.

SECTION 2
RAISE AWARENESS

Raise Awareness – Introduction

Raising awareness of inclusion and diversity within your organisation is essential. It's important that everyone understands their roles in and contribution to building an inclusive culture.

A study conducted by People Management concluded that inclusion and diversity have a better chance of being implemented and embedded within an organisation when the task does not sit purely with HR.[13] I could not agree more. It's not, however, something that can be added to somebody's job description. It's not one line in an annual report, and it's not just the annual submission of gender pay. I firmly believe that in order for an organisation to create an inclusive workplace culture, everyone must take responsibility. While it needs to be championed at the highest level,

---

13 https://www.peoplemanagement.co.uk/news/articles/
    diversity-initiatives-successful-moved-out-hr-report

I firmly believe that the whole workforce must be involved.

In this section, I'll share some steps you can take to raise awareness within your organisation about the importance of inclusion and diversity and we'll explore the following areas:

- **Credible leaders** – the importance of having visible and credible leaders who will become your champions for diversity and inclusion. These individuals need to truly believe in the benefits that an inclusive and diverse organisation brings.

- **Unconscious bias** – we'll learn what unconscious biases are and what impact they have on decisions made during activities such as recruitment, selection, performance reviews and talent planning.

- **Health and wellbeing** – we'll learn how an inclusive workplace culture can positively impact on the health of your workforce.

- **Communication** – consider the language and tone you use within your organisation when you communicate with your employees.

- **Employee engagement** – we'll learn about the benefits of having an engaged workforce and why it's important to have a process in place to check how satisfied and engaged your workforce feels.

– **Company values** – You'll be encouraged to reflect upon your company values. Are they sufficiently compelling for employees, customers and stakeholders to want to align with them?

By the time you've finished this section of the book, my hope is that you'll understand that creating an inclusive workplace culture is not just about one or two individuals undertaking a few initiatives, but that it takes the whole workforce to close the gap together. Let's get started on the next stage of the tribe5 Diversity & Inclusion methodology: **raising awareness** of the importance of inclusion and diversity.

Raise Awareness – Credible Leaders

When you're building an inclusive culture, it's important to have credible senior management who truly believe in the value a diverse workforce can bring. The leadership team sits in a privileged position, setting the tone and direction of the organisation. People look to senior management as role models and will follow their lead.

It's important to have an influential figurehead / senior executive within the organisation who will champion diversity and inclusion. So, what does it take to be an inclusive leader?

Well, in my experience an inclusive leader is someone who:

- Wholeheartedly believes everyone is equal
- Understands what an inclusive workplace culture looks and feels like
- Is motivated to accelerate progress and will promote new strategies and policies
- Is committed and will hold others to account when they fall short of the required standards and behaviours

Is this you? Do you see others demonstrating some or all of these qualities? I hope so, as we need to see more leaders role-modelling these characteristics.

Leadership influence and managing change

When you're building an inclusive and diverse workforce, it may be necessary to bring about a significant culture change. Leadership influence is particularly critical at such times. Employees will look at the behaviour and actions of you and your senior team to see how you are responding and follow your lead. Your every move will be scrutinised, so the way in which you behave as you build your inclusive culture will have a direct correlation to the success of the change.

Therefore, everyone who chooses to be a leader has a special obligation to be aware of the influence and impact they have on people and situations. When you're a leader within an organisation, you can't easily separate your personal life from your professional life – you are a role model 100% of the time.

The importance of personal awareness is huge within a leadership position. I work with many leadership teams. Some individuals have a high degree of self-awareness. They understand who they are. They recognise their behaviours. They are aware of their biases and understand the impact that their leadership behaviour has on others. There are, however, some leaders who have very poor self-awareness. They have a one-dimensional perspective of leadership, ie their own view of the world! They rarely have the desire or ability to step into the shoes of someone else.

You can use psychometric and personality profiling tools as a reference point for members of a leadership team to fully understand themselves and their impact on others. I'm accredited to use a variety of profiling instruments, but my tool of choice is Insights Discovery. It provides a simple yet effective framework based on Jung's theory and highlights energy preferences and traits through a colour system. The ease of application of the Insights Discovery tool enables individuals to quickly grasp their own traits and those of their colleagues. For leaders, it helps them identify their leadership, decision making and communication style. To learn more about the Insights Discovery tool, visit: https://www.junglehr.com/bespoke_programmes_training/insights-discovery/

Leadership effectiveness

Leaders who build inclusive workplace cultures consistently demonstrate inclusive leadership behaviours. But what are these? Let's take a look.

Caring about others. Inclusive leaders care about those who work for their organisation. They are available for individuals as well as the team. By this, I don't just mean that they leave their office door open; I mean that they proactively take the time to get to know and understand everyone who is part of their team. They are easy to talk to, and they're willing to set time aside to listen to what employees have to say and give them their undivided attention.

Curiosity. An inclusive leader has an unquenchable thirst for learning. They're always open to new ideas and new ways of doing things, and they recognise the value that a diverse workforce brings because of the different ideas it generates. They encourage the sharing of experiences to enable growth and development not only of the business, but also of the people who operate within it.

Vulnerability. An inclusive leader recognises their own abilities, skills and strengths, so they are not afraid to be vulnerable. They are prepared to share their hopes, fears, desires and concerns. They will reach out for help when they find a gap in their knowledge, recognising that others may hold expertise that they don't currently possess. An inclusive leader is open and willing to allow opportunities for others to step into their brilliance.

Fairness and equity. An inclusive leader understands the importance of treating staff fairly. They don't operate a system which allows favouritism. A leader who operates in an inclusive culture is in tune with any minority groups and will act as a role model to encourage others to step up and contribute to the organisation's goals.

An inclusive leader will also champion suggestions and ideas from others. They will facilitate the actions needed to progress initiatives which could otherwise get stuck in a bottleneck. Inclusive leaders cannot be everywhere or manage everyone, so they will empower others to make decisions too.

Trust

Trust is an important component for everyone. It's the foundation of strong relationships. However, pinpointing specifically what we mean by trust can be hard to do.

When working with executive boards and leadership teams, I encourage them to consider the Trust Equation. This sets out a formula to help individuals with their decision making. The three elements, credibility, reliability and intimacy, need to be increased to build trust, balanced by self-orientation.

This is the trust equation.

$$\text{Trust} = \frac{\text{Credibility} + \text{Reliability} + \text{Intimacy}}{\text{Self-orientation}}$$

Leaders are trusted with credibility through their qualifications, experience and position within the organisation. Reliability is about delivering on commitments and promises. Intimacy is around confidentiality and whether leaders can be trusted with information about an individual. Self-orientation is about whether the leader has an individual's best interests at heart, or are they only interested in advancing their own career or getting a job done regardless of the consequences?

By considering each element of the Trust Equation, leaders can be clear about which component they may be lacking. Inclusive leaders are genuinely interested in others. They treat every group and individual fairly. They honour their commitments, take the time to build solid relationships, truly understand and value the unique differences that individuals bring, and recognise the diversity that people bring collectively.

Polarities of leadership

The agility that leaders now require becomes even more apparent when they're managing their own needs as well as the polarities of their employees. This continual balancing act can create conflict and tension at times for a leader, particularly when they are asked to:

– Be the voice of the employees while interpreting leadership decisions

– Be both an advocate for employees and for managers

- Build and strengthen relationships while enforcing leadership decisions

- Manage change while focusing on the delivery of tasks

Raising awareness – Credible leaders summary

Inclusive leadership isn't just something you do occasionally when someone is watching. Inclusive leadership isn't a task – it's a way of being.

Ryan Jenkins, millennial and generation Z speaker, sums it up in his article '6 Questions That Reveal If You Are an Inclusive Leader':

'Inclusive leaders not only embrace, value and provide a sense of belonging to individuals, but they leverage differences as competitive advantage.'[14]

Reflect now on how credible your leadership style is in a world of inclusion and diversity, and follow the advice in this chapter to fill in any gaps.

---

14 www.inc.com/ryan-jenkins/how-to-be-an-inclusive-leader-in-6-steps.html

Raise Awareness –
Unconscious Bias

'Unconscious bias' is a phrase you're likely to have heard, but what does it mean? Are we really aware of the prejudices we act upon each and every day?

Unconscious bias is created and influenced by our feelings as well as our rational thought processes. Our personal experience, background, education and cultural environment can all contribute to the often deep-seated prejudices we hold. In short, our brains make quick judgements and assessments of others without us even being aware of it.

While unconscious biases are natural, it's important to say that most don't come from a place of bad intent. However, they can have huge implications not only in our own lives, but in the lives of others too.

In truth, I'm conscious that this book has a bias. My bias, of course, is towards closing the gender gap for women. My own life experience prejudices my bias and fuels my desire to be an advocate for others. To reach back and push forward. To play my role in increasing the presence of women in senior leadership roles within organisations. To ensure that organisations build cultures that are great places in which to work so that my children and grandchildren will be able to step into their brilliance.

However, I'm also sufficiently aware of my own biases. Having spent many years in the field of inclusivity and diversity, I recognise that it's greater than gender. I'm a strong advocate and ambassador for others, recognising the value that everyone's unique differences bring.

What is unconscious bias?

When you're creating an inclusive workplace culture, it's important to understand that biases do exist, particularly as most of us believe that we are ethical and unbiased. Researcher Mahzarin R. Banaji, in a *Harvard Business Review* article 'How (Un)ethical Are You?', stated, '*In reality, most of us fall woefully short of our inflated self-perception*'.[15] Whether we are aware of it or not, these perceptions affect our judgement and our decision making.

---

15   https://hbr.org/2003/12/how-unethical-are-you

In the article '9 Types of Unconscious Bias and the Shocking Ways They Affect Your Recruiting Efforts' (November 3rd 2016), Siofra Pratt identifies that when making recruitment decisions biases can affect such things as:

- The way in which we interpret reality and see others – our perception

- How we react when interacting with others – our attitude

- How welcoming we are towards others – our behaviours

- What attributes of others are we drawn towards – our attention

- How well we listen to what others say – our listening skills

- The way in which we tune into others wellbeing – our advocacy

- Our micro-affirmations – how much or how little we comfort certain people in certain situations[16]

When we're building an inclusive workplace culture, it's important to tune into the biases that individuals may hold and help them to understand the impact these may have on others. These biases can include:

---

16 https://www.socialtalent.com/blog/recruitment/9-types-of-bias

- **Beauty bias** – forming an opinion or placing a value judgement on what we see and how someone looks. If an individual looks somehow different, then they may be overlooked.

- **Confirmation bias** – searching for something within that individual that backs up any first impressions (good or bad) we have formed.

- **Affinity bias** – favouring someone or aligning ourselves with someone who we feel is the same as us. In recruitment terms, this is akin to saying someone is a good 'cultural fit'.

- **Attribution bias** – our perception of the actions of others, eg when they have done something well it's because they are lucky. However, when they have done something badly, it's as a result of their personality, behaviour or socio-economic background (which may be different to our own).

- **Conformity bias** – swaying and influencing the views and opinions of others to match ours so we 'fit in'.

- **Horns effect** – making negative judgements about an individual or an aspect of their character which we don't like. Allowing this to cloud our judgement.

- **Halo effect** – holding a belief about a great feature in an individual. This could be their attendance at a prestigious further education establishment or the attainment of a particular grade.

Business award bias

Here's a personal story I wish to share with you about unconscious bias.

I was absolutely thrilled to have reached the finals of a business award. The next stage of the process was to attend a panel interview. I recall standing in front of the judging panel, which comprised both male and female members, delivering my business presentation in the allotted time. Then it was time for questions.

The first question came from the head judge (who was male). 'What does your husband do?' he asked. I remember being dumbfounded by the question. It was totally irrelevant to my presentation, yet I found myself answering in a reactionary manner. I shared my husband's profession with him in response to his question, and I recall him replying, 'So your husband's the main breadwinner then. You're playing at business.' None of the other panel members challenged the relevance or appropriateness of that question.

Afterwards, I became so cross with myself that I'd answered that question. I had been stunned by it, yet I'd found myself compliantly answering. I should have challenged back and asked for clarification as to the relevance of the question.

This is a prime example of unconscious bias. Not one member of that panel challenged the appropriateness of the question. And in truth, I must acknowledge my part too as I was complicit by answering. There won't be a next, that's for sure!

It's called 'unconscious' bias for a reason. Even those who are highly attuned to their thoughts and beliefs may experience a lapse and have a negative opinion towards others, so it's important to raise awareness within your workforce. Call out when instances of unconscious bias occur and ensure that any prejudices don't stray into discrimination.

Prejudice vs discrimination

One of the most outspoken figures, who is still advocating for people to think of themselves as part of the human race and not any particular race or characteristic, is Jane Elliott (https://janeelliott.com/). In 1970, she famously divided a class of (all white) schoolchildren into eye colour – brown eyes and blue eyes. She told them that brown-eyed people were smarter, faster and better. By the end of the day, the brown-eyed children were displaying confidence and even some aggressive tendencies, whereas the blue-eyed children became timid and despondent.

What Elliott said she learned from the exercise was that people are not born prejudiced, but learn the behaviour. And if it can be learned, she said, it can be unlearned.

'Prejudice is an attitude. It can't hurt anyone.
But discrimination is a behaviour, and people
get killed because of it every day.'
— Jane Elliott

Fifty years later, we're perhaps more aware than ever
that discrimination in the workplace is unacceptable.
Most companies will put managers through formal
training to ensure that they are aware of how and
when discrimination can occur. But is this enough and
does it work?

Training is important when we're building an inclusive workplace culture, but opening up discussions
so people really understand what life is like within a
particular organisation is key – this can include providing a platform for individuals to be able to share
openly and for others to understand the implications
of unintentional actions or decisions. This also include
the apparently benign act of allocating of work with
the intention of making someone's life easier. While
these intentions might be honourable, they could in
fact erode that person's confidence or reduce their
career advancement opportunities.

Campaigns such as #PurpleLightUp, which celebrates
World Disabled Day, International Women's Day,
International Men's Day, #MeToo and Pride Month
use social movements and networks to build awareness and shift mindsets. Things are changing, albeit
slowly. Often within families, children are more open

to differences in people than their parents and grand-parents were.

Unconscious bias training doesn't work

I'd love to say it does, (and you might be expecting me to say it does) but research from Frank Dobbin of Harvard, Alexandra Kalev of Berkeley, and Erin Kelly of the University of Minnesota shows us that manda-tory unconscious bias training, when it's delivered as a standalone module, doesn't actually work.[17] Despite millions being spent on 'diversity training', attitudes and the diversity of organisations have stayed the same.

The researchers concluded that:

'In firms where training is mandatory or emphasises the threat of lawsuits, training actually has negative effects on management diversity.'

CASE STUDY – ONE DAY IS NOT ENOUGH

At the start of its inclusion journey, the board of a law firm believed it would be beneficial to raise awareness of the unconscious bias of its

---

17 https://scholar.harvard.edu/dobbin/files/2007_contexts_dobbin_kalev_kelly.pdf

partners and senior management and invested in a full day's training programme and engaged an external provider to deliver this. The first half of the workshop was setting the scene and highlighting what unconscious biases were, with the second half allowing reflective practice in terms of how they played out within the organisation. No follow-up training was offered, nor was this awareness training part of an inclusion strategy or woven into the firm's wider inclusion journey.

Many partners left feeling frustrated at the end of the workshop, having lost a day's valuable work. They reported being no further forward in terms of their knowledge and thinking about how to tackle unconscious bias; the session only served to highlight the consequences of their continued behaviour. If anything, it reinforced some of the unconscious bias practices that were already taking place in the firm.

Using other senses

Just think how much more powerful we could be if we made decisions without bias and used our other senses. Here are two great examples.

In the 1970s and 1980s, the top five orchestras in the US were made up of less than 5 per cent women.[18] To

18 www.theguardian.com/women-in-leadership/2013/oct/14/blind-auditions-orchestras-gender-bias

understand if their selection was affected through bias the orchestras decided to hold blind music auditions. Screens were placed on the stage and candidates were asked to perform behind them for the selection panel. In some instances, blind auditions were only used for the preliminary audition, whereas in others they were continued right through until the hiring decision was made. As a consequence, the musicians were selected on their ability as opposed to their look or their gender, race, age, faith or disability.

In some respects, we have the modern-day version of that in the BBC TV programme *The Voice*. The judges have no idea what the individuals look like, so they listen to the sound of their voices and make their choices in accordance with that.

Raise awareness – Unconscious bias summary

When you're starting out on your inclusion journey, it is important to acknowledge that unconscious biases do exist. They've been forming in people's brains for years through their life experiences and socio environments. To surface these biases, you can provide platforms for individuals to raise their awareness and understand the impact they have.

These can involve:

- Enabling individuals to work alongside a diverse range of people as equals. This helps promote social accountability and allows employees to have the opportunity to step into another individual's shoes and to experience what life is like for them.

- Educating people about stereotypes. Highlight when these might occur in the workplace, such as during recruitment, performance reviews or talent planning.

- Making unconscious bias training voluntary and weaving this into a wider programme around inclusion.

- Having open conversations. Provide safe spaces for people to share their experiences and an opportunity to give feedback.

- Having diversity in your management and leadership teams.

- Reaching out to the local communities in which you operate and becoming part of these communities. Understand their challenges and work with these communities to build creative solutions to overcome these challenges.

- Setting up diversity councils or forums: a task force of employees and managers to provide focus on diversity and inclusion.

- Make diversity and inclusion the responsibility of all individuals and not just senior managers.

Bias cannot be avoided. It can affect decision making within the workplace, from recruitment and performance discussions through to talent planning. However, raising awareness can move your organisation towards ensuring implicit biases are kept at bay. It won't be easy, and it won't happen overnight. It'll take real commitment and resources.

 You'll need to:

- Understand where bias is coming from

- Challenge others about how they are making decisions and what they are basing their decision on

- Avoid getting swept along by others or excluding individuals because they don't look the same as you or share your beliefs

- Recognise that there are positive and negative biases – a negative bias could be 'men are better in the boardroom than women', a positive bias could be that 'exercise is better than a diet'

- Have accessible role models to counterbalance stereotypes, such as male nurses or female pilots

By including everyone on the diversity journey, you're much more likely to surface any biases that your people hold. In doing so, you'll raise awareness of unconscious bias within your organisation and create an inclusive culture.

Raise Awareness – Health And Wellbeing

A healthy workforce is good for business. However, it's often a taboo subject. Many managers feel that enquiring about the health of an individual is straying into a 'nanny state' culture. Others avoid discussions with their team members because they either don't want to be drawn into someone's personal life, or fear they could be accused of straying into subject areas which may result in accusations of discriminatory practice. As such, the topic of health and wellbeing is often skirted around and left in the 'too difficult' pile.

However, when you're building an inclusive work-place culture, it's important to understand the health of your workforce and tackle any underlying factors. The aim for any organisation should be to create a working environment where everyone's aware of unwanted behaviour – where individuals are, free from unnecessary pressures, and where every individual is treated with respect and dignity.

Here are a few places where you can explore the health and wellbeing of your employees.

24/7

Technology can play an important role in providing flexible working solutions. It can also increase business efficiencies. There are, however, some downsides to the advancement of technology.

While greater interconnectivity provides business opportunities on a global scale, it can also mean that we are potentially (or need to be) available 24/7. This has led to an increase of pressure on employees who struggle to switch off. I for one am guilty of this – the inability to resist sneaking a peak at emails. The feeling that each email I receive requires an immediate response. The constant demand to be available to deal with a manager's requests or client queries. This, along with other workplace factors, can result in burnout and stress-related symptoms.

A labour agreement was introduced in France in 2016 which gave all employees who worked for a company which employed over fifty workers the right to 'disconnect'. This initiative prevented employees from either receiving or feeling compelled to respond to company communications during the evening and weekends. It was intended to go some way towards addressing a culture of permanent connection and reduce work–home encroachment.[19]

But this is not the first time we've seen such measures being put into place. In 2011 Volkswagen agreed to deactivate the technology devices of workers after hours to avoid them being pestered by emails.[20] In the US an insurance company is reported to have given its workers sleep monitors, with the promise of a financial incentive if they got twenty consecutive nights of good sleep.[21]

The Law Society at the Inter-Law Diversity Forum event, which I attended in December 2018, reported the demands placed upon lawyers within the working environment it had itself created. It has had a standard growing practice where billable hours were its primary focus, and client demands and workflow resulted in a culture of long hours. The Law Society has now signed up to initiatives such as the Mindful Business Charter in recognition of the toll this culture was taking on the welfare and wellbeing of those who had to operate within it.

19 www.bbc.co.uk/news/magazine-36249647
20 https://thenextweb.com/world/2017/01/02/
    french-workers-neglect-work-email/
21 www.bbc.co.uk/news/magazine-36249647

The Mindful Business Charter has been developed by the UK's biggest banks, alongside law firms with a shared agenda for supporting mental health and wellbeing within the workplace. The charter acknowledges the changing working culture and details a set of principles which focus on the improvement of communication, respect for rest periods, and appropriate delegation of tasks.

Details of the charter can be found at www.mind.org.uk.

Mental health

The previously unspoken issue of mental health has been quite rightly highlighted and brought out into the open by high-profile individuals, including members of the UK royal family. Prince Harry's openness about his personal struggles has helped thousands of individuals to recognise that mental health issues are not only real, but can affect anyone at any time.

Conditions associated with mental health can go undetected for years. They can lie dormant and are often masked by individuals who are suffering, as was the case with the actor Robin Williams. To the outside world, he presented as an outgoing and jovial comedian, while internally he was battling with depression, which ultimately resulted in him taking his own life.

Unlike other health conditions, you can't always recognise who might be experiencing challenges with mental health. Yet it's very real. The effects can be devastating not only for the sufferer, but also for their friends, colleagues and loved ones.

However, help is at hand. Mental health first aid is now widely available. This training can ensure that managers are appropriately equipped not only to spot the signs, but also to offer support to those who may require help. Acknowledging mental health as a condition which may affect your workforce and putting measures in place to ensure those who are suffering get the support they need is vital for building an inclusive workplace culture.

Further information on mental health can be obtained from www.nhs.uk/conditions/stress-anxiety-depression/mental-health-helplines/ and www.mind.org.uk/

Stress and anxiety

It's good to have a bit of stress. In fact, some people thrive under the pressure of working right up to the wire and often deliver their best work at the last minute. However, too much stress or prolonged periods of pressure can adversely affect our health.

In the *Embed – The Role Of Communication* chapter, we'll explore how, through the use of personality profiling tools such as Insights Discovery, individuals can understand what happens to their behaviour when they are having 'bad days', or learn to spot the signs in others. By having this level of awareness, individuals can take measures to identify and reduce the causes of stress. If they see the signs in colleagues, they can take the necessary steps to support them.

 Additional ways to combat stress can include:

- Ensuring that individuals fully understand the role and responsibility of the job they are expected to perform

- Making sure that deadlines are realistic and achievable

- Offering support and encouragement

- Empowering staff to make their own decisions

- Getting to know your team – allow reflection/ thinking time for those who don't like to be put on the spot

- Making sure that your workforce has sufficient rest time. Review holiday requests – have they been fairly allocated? Has everyone taken their annual leave entitlement?

- Tuning into your workforce – have you noticed a change in behaviour among your team members?

Work with your HR department to understand if there are any underlying employee relation issues.

 Take a moment to consider:

- What does your people data tell you about levels of sickness absence within your organisation?

- What are the reasons employees give for their absences?

- Have any complaints been raised? How have these been addressed? Do they highlight any underlying problems with management capability which require addressing and/or additional training?

Stress among your workforce can cost your organisations thousands of pounds. By raising awareness of the impact that stress can have on your employees and putting measures in place to support those who may be experiencing stress in the workplace, you will support your journey to building a more inclusive environment.

Postnatal depression

Pregnancy and childbirth can have many side effects for women. Due to changes in hormone levels, women may experience symptoms of morning sickness, heartburn and leg cramps during pregnancy (I can speak from experience). Following the birth of the baby, side effects may include exhaustion from lack of sleep (I speak from experience on this point too).

Many new mothers also experience low moods after giving birth. These symptoms often lessen and disappear after a short period of time, but for some women, postnatal depression can become a long-term problem if left untreated. Postnatal depression affects women in different ways, so encourage those experiencing symptoms to seek professional help as soon as possible.

It's important to recognise that postnatal depression can affect dads too. The National Childbirth Trust is the UK's largest parent charity and reported that 'the number of men who became depressed in the first year after becoming a dad is double that of the general population'. Postnatal depression in fathers can show itself in different ways, yet many men report feeling unable to tell anyone that they feel overwhelmed or anxious when they become new fathers.[22]

Encouragingly, in December 2018, the British National Health Service (NHS) announced that partners of new and expectant mothers will be offered a comprehensive mental health assessment and signposted to professional support if needed.

---

22 www.nct.org.uk/life-parent/dads-and-partners/
postnatal-depression-dads-10-things-you-should-know

Employee assistance programmes

An employee assistance programme (EAP) is a benefits programme offered by many organisations. Through a range of confidential support programmes, an EAP is able to assist employees with personal or work-related problems which may be impacting on their job performance, mental health and overall emotional wellbeing. Services include short-term counselling, support around relationship, financial, drug and alcohol concerns, and legal issues.

EAP schemes can sometimes be offered as a standalone benefit, or they could be offered to employees via other benefits such as private healthcare schemes. Whichever route you choose, it's important to ensure that all employees know that the EAP exists and how it can be accessed.

If you don't already offer an EAP, then you may wish to address this within your inclusion strategy. Employees who feel safe and supported within a work environment are much more able to perform at their best.

Diet

Health and wellbeing can be supported/enhanced through the food choices employees make. If it's not possible for your organisation to offer onsite catering facilities, you may wish to consider what self-catering provisions you are able to offer, such as microwaves and kettles. For health and safety reasons, some organisations are unable to provide these, and therefore rely on third-party providers such as external caterers. These caterers may visit your site in a mobile kitchen, or you may have vending machines which are stocked daily. If third-party catering is something you offer to your employees, then make sure you work proactively with your suppliers to ensure the food they offer is healthy and affordable.

If your company is able to offer onsite restaurant facilities, again work with your catering team to ensure that the meals they offer are healthy. It's important to recognise that individuals may have dietary requirements, so food labelling is very important, as is the provision for a broad range of dietary needs.

Some companies are able to subsidise their restaurant facility. This can be of great benefit to employees as affordability for many can play a factor in the food choices which they make.

Whichever solution you offer, it's important to ensure that employees take their rest breaks, and that they keep themselves hydrated and power up their minds through healthy eating. You might wish to encourage your employees to have their lunch away from their desks. Sharing meals together can be an invaluable time for teams to bond or networking to occur, and an opportunity for leadership teams to be visible. Hosting cultural-themed food events can be a great way to bring people together, providing a platform to educate others on different beliefs through a shared experience of food.

Respect

Maintaining transparent rules regarding workplace bullying and harassment is just one of the things you can do to create a respectful workplace. Make sure that everyone understands the procedure to follow if they do wish to raise any concerns. Clearly set out what the investigation process looks like. It's important that employees know that the company takes complaints seriously and perpetrators will be held to account for any wrongdoing.

In *Raise Awareness – Company Values*, we will explore company values in more detail, but simply setting out how you expect your employees to behave sets the tone for the culture of your organisation.

 Here are just a few things you can do:

– Ensure managers role model the right behaviours

– Get to know your workforce – go out of your way to learn the names of employees

– Listen to employees – give them your undivided attention

– Show courtesy by allowing everyone an opportunity to speak and contribute to meetings or discussions

– Call out unacceptable behaviour

– Help individuals to understand how their behaviour or actions impact others

If everyone is respectful and courteous towards each other, your organisation's culture will be transformed.

Healthcare

Unfortunately, illness can arise and may require professional intervention. The provision of healthcare can therefore aid employee wellbeing, particularly if treatment can be expedited through a private medical system.

Some organisations provide access to private medical schemes as part of their remuneration packages. We explored this in *Take Stock – Reward and Remuneration* as it requires careful consideration to ensure that such schemes are offered on a fair and equitable basis.

Where it's not possible for you to fund a private healthcare scheme, you may wish to explore a 'pay as you go' scheme, often funded via salary sacrifice arrangements. These schemes can offer the opportunity for all employees to purchase healthcare cover for themselves and their families at a discounted price, should they wish.

Getting active

Encouraging employees to participate in physical activity is great for increasing the health and wellbeing of your workforce. This could include having an onsite gym, or where that isn't possible, partnering with local gyms to provide discounted corporate membership.

Schemes such as the Cycle to Work Scheme, introduced by the UK government in 1999, are intended to promote healthier journeys to work while reducing environmental pollution. The scheme makes it possible for individuals to have access to bikes and accessories for an agreed length of time. Guidance on how to implement a scheme can be found at www.gov.uk/ government/publications/cycle-to-work-scheme-implementation-guidance. Another consideration is to explore what facilities are available at the workplace, such safe spaces for employees to leave their bikes and showers to enable them to freshen up when they arrive at work.

In my early career, one organisation invited a fitness instructor onsite weekly to run an exercise class after work in the restaurant area (with the tables cleared away, of course). Some employees get together and organise running clubs, which may meet during lunch breaks or after work. Others like to hold 'walking meetings' where they head outside for a stroll around the block while discussing the business.

Getting active and moving is important for wellbeing, so we need to support employees to make it part of their daily lives. Here's a case study to show you how.

CASE STUDY - PROJECT ZOLA

As part of an executive coaching programme, a senior partner identified that he wanted to enhance his leadership effectiveness. He recognised that due to the long hours he was working, he didn't always take the time to look after himself from a health and diet perspective. He wasn't eating properly and would often snack at his desk. He rarely had time to exercise and had observed that his suits were getting tighter. He also recognised that his energy levels were low, and at times he was irritable with his team.

During the coaching session, we explored ways in which he could take some positive action to change things. One of the things he said he wanted to do was to go back to the gym as it was something which he had previously enjoyed, but he felt that he now didn't have the time.

His diary was visible for everyone to see, and while this was great and transparent in terms of where he was, it meant that any 'keep free' times were often disregarded. He also reported that he would feel guilty about putting 'gym' in his diary as he should be doing other 'more important' things.

This led us on to discussions about the importance of his health and wellbeing and his ability to operate at optimum level. We talked about how he managed other tasks that needed to be completed and delivered against. The result of this coaching session was that he gave his fitness campaign the name 'Project Zola' and booked the time in his diary under the project name rather than 'gym'. By making it into a project, he felt able to accept taking the time to get fit.

While Project Zola wasn't a secret, it created an air of mystery. Everyone who had access to his diary respected the time which was allocated to Project Zola, and within a short period of time, the senior partner was enjoying positive physical and behavioural changes.

Raising awareness – Health and wellbeing summary

Health is a gift which we can sometimes take for granted. It's often not until our health suffers that we pay attention to it. I for one am guilty of paying attention to my health only when I feel unwell, instead of giving thanks for the healthy life I've been blessed with (note to self – I need to pay more attention to this).

For many individuals, however, living with poor health or a disability is something they have to do every day. Health issues can arise at any point in our lives. They can be triggered by life events, lifestyle choices, or genetics and aging. We can be impacted by our own ill health, the ill health of a family member or friend. What is guaranteed is that at some point in our lives, we will all come into contact with someone who has experienced ill health and/or see the devastating effects it can have.

The health and wellbeing of your workforce are paramount. Having a healthy workforce will set the tone for the health of your business. Raising awareness about this important topic within your organisation will help your employees to feel safe to speak out, reach out for help and support each other.

Raise Awareness –
Employee Engagement And
Recognition

Employee engagement has become an ubiquitous buzz phrase. Although the exact definition remains elusive, through an amalgamation of research, I understand employee engagement to be an approach adopted within the workplace whereby employees feel committed to the goals and values of the business, and motivated to contribute to the organisation's success. An engaged employee is likely to be one who is fully absorbed and enthusiastic about not only their work, but also the company and its values.

Why is employee engagement important?

According to Gallup's 2017 State of the Global Workforce Survey,[23] workplaces which have the most engaged employees reported:

- 41% less absenteeism
- 24% less staff turnover
- 21% greater profitability
- 17% greater productivity

Engaged employees put in what is called 'discretionary effort' over and above what they have to do to get their pay. When an organisation's employees are engaged, relationships around them are strengthened, they have a greater sense of collaboration and teamwork, and they take pride in what they're doing.

Having a shared purpose is important. A good organisation will be clear on its values and the direction it's travelling – this requires strong and inspirational leadership. It's also important that employees feel able to make decisions. To do this, you can provide a simple structure that draws feedback from across the company. Once you've reflected upon what you've learned through the feedback, share with the business what you plan to do differently as a result. A great example of sharing is

---

23 www.gallup.com/workplace/238079/state-global-workplace-2017.aspx

to report back to the employees in a 'You said'… 'We did' style, giving them examples of improvements or changes you've made because of their feedback.

All of the above are great ways of focusing on employee engagement as part of your strategy for building an inclusive workplace culture. However, organisations often don't know where to start, so here are some top tips.

How do you make a workplace great?

 Having worked for one of the *Sunday Times* 'Top 100 Best Companies to Work For' and been responsible for its Great Place to Work programme, I know only too well the benefits an engaged workforce can bring. By having a framework and action plan the company I worked for increased its ranking year on year.

Frameworks, such as those provided by Best Companies or Great Place to Work not only provide a structure, but give you useful data to enable you to assess where your organisation is at present. You can use this information to benchmark your business and set objectives for the areas that you need to focus and improve on. Capturing this information is really important, but it doesn't have to be onerous. You could do it via a spreadsheet or the use of technology such as planning tools like Asana, Trello, Basecamp, Evernote or Google Drive.

The most important thing is to capture where you are at present, where you wish to be, and the actions that you intend to take. But don't formulate your plan in isolation. You can't achieve a great place to work alone. It's important to engage the workforce widely in the creation of a plan so that they feel involved, can take ownership and celebrate the changes as the business moves forward.

From my own experience, I set up a Great Place to Work team of individuals from various parts of the business who had varying degrees of engagement. Some individuals demonstrated a high degree of alignment with the company's values and were already offering impressive levels of discretionary effort. However, I balanced the team by involving those who weren't currently valuing all the company was able to offer. They were invited to join the Great Place to Work team as they had a different view of the company and an equally important contribution to make. This was an opportunity not just to influence their thinking, but also to ensure that the company wasn't looking at the business through rose-tinted glasses and embarking upon a journey that not everyone felt committed to.

If you provide training to leadership teams, you will help them to understand the importance of employee engagement. Focus this training not only on what employee engagement is, but also on the contribution that your leaders and managers make in building an engaged workforce.

Communicate your plan

Once you have proposed an engagement plan, the next step is to share it within your business. This isn't a singular activity and it shouldn't be top secret. Through the creation of a robust internal communications plan, you can update your employees regularly.

A communication plan doesn't need to be complex, but it does need to include multiple channels so that you engage with a wide audience. Consider activities such as sharing stories and celebrating achievements via a newsletter, on the internet or at regular company briefings. Make the communication plan two-way, and ensure that whatever communication activity you choose, you do it consistently.

You can find more details on how to build an effective internal communication plan and access a simple but effective leadership communication plan by visiting www.JungleHR.com.

Make your leaders accessible

The 'Great Place to Work for Women' 2018 report (which can be downloaded for free at https://www. greatplacetowork.com/resources/reports/best-workplaces-for-women-list-one-page-key-findings-report-landing-page) found that accessible line managers and role models are key factors in creating a great place to work. In the *Inspire and Involve – Role Models* section we explore further the importance of accessible role models when creating an inclusive culture.

Redefine your company vison and values

Leaders and line managers should fully understand the company values and demonstrate them positively and proactively through their leadership behaviours.

When you're looking at employee engagement within your organisation, it's important to revisit your mission and vision. As well as highlighting what you do as an organisation, your mission and vision statements need to inspire individuals to feel passionate about being part of that journey.

 Take a moment to consider:

– Do you place people at the centre of your organisation?

– Is there an opportunity for individuals to make a difference?

In 2015, United Nations leaders came together to agree seventeen Global Goals for a Better World by

2030.[24] These goals have the power to address some of the world's biggest problems such as ending poverty, fighting inequality and combating climate change.

Every organisation has an opportunity to make a difference in the world and can align itself with at least one of the United Nations Global Goals. Many individuals have personal desires and aspirations to make a difference to the world they live in and which they will leave for future generations. When an organisation focuses on aligning the business with such a purpose over and above profit, it will increase employee engagement, particularly when the purpose is aligned with the values of staff members.

Charities such as B1G1 provide a platform and frame-work for organisations to commence purposeful, charitable activities if they don't currently operate them. Further information can be found at https://www.b1g1.com/businessforgood/

Promote a work-life balance

I for one enjoy working. I enjoy the intellectual stimulation and the camaraderie that working with clients on their projects can bring, but I don't want to do it all the time. I also enjoy the ability to work in a flexible way so that I can spend time with my family, explore the world and take time out to rest, relax and recharge.

---

24 www.globalgoals.org

And so I believe it's important for our wellbeing to have a degree of work-life balance.

You can achieve this in the working environment by having robust and engaging policies and procedures. The right policies will enable your workforce to achieve a work-life balance while remaining sufficiently motivated to produce the outcomes and performance required for the business. When an organisation focuses on performance as opposed to presenteeism, this goes some way towards achieving a positive work-life balance.

Gather feedback regularly

To be clear, I think employee engagement surveys are helpful. However, they're only a snapshot of a particular moment in time, painting a historic picture of what it was like to work for your company on that particular day.

What can be more helpful is to examine the information year on year and combine it with initiatives that check in regularly with your employees. Examples include monthly or weekly one-to-one meetings with managers or leadership sessions. You can also share information through employee forums, as well as using technology such as real-time 'pulse' apps which enable employees to give 'in the moment' feedback. This level of information will enable you to understand your people and be in tune with them in real time, making changes when necessary.

Recognition schemes

It's also important to celebrate successes along the way. This builds employee engagement and makes people feel proud of the organisation for which they work. Make this celebration visual. Display something around the office or on people's desks, or reward employees with certificates or cards.

CASE STUDY – SHINE

A manufacturing organisation, which is ranked as a Best Company to Work For, introduced an employee recognition scheme as part of its employee engagement strategy. The company wanted an opportunity for every employee to shine, so it introduced a recognition scheme and called it SHINE.

S – straightforward. Everything the company did had to be jargon free: the way that they communicated with the employees and the customers. Everything needed to be easy to understand and informative, not intimidating. The vocabulary needed to be straightforward so as not to exclude individuals who didn't share particular knowledge or understanding.

H – helpful. The company leaders wanted to make sure individuals always offered support to each other when required. The leaders were responsible for checking in with the business and its people regularly to ensure they were setting employees up for success, that employees had the right tools and talent to perform effectively, and that they were empowered to make decisions.

I – innovation. Part of the company's engagement strategy focused on continuous improvement – the ability for all employees to spot opportunities for development. The business leaders recognised that often the best people to spot those opportunities were on the ground, operating in the business every day. As a consequence, they introduced a scheme whereby employees were able to offer suggestions for consideration. Either these were then implemented, or the leaders provided feedback, thanking staff for their contribution and explaining why it may not be possible to implement their suggestion at that time. The business leaders also celebrated the innovative ideas that staff had put forward, ensuring that those who had made suggestions were recognised and involved in the implementation of their ideas where appropriate.

N – no limits to customer service. Customer service didn't just sit within the customer experience team, but was the responsibility of all employees. Everyone became customers of each other. Service levels improved as everyone shared knowledge and information, and worked proactively across departments to lend a hand at busy times.

E – empower and engage. The organisation recognised that the management of people makes all the difference. In order for them to do their job properly to the best of their ability, employees have to feel empowered to do the right thing. This required the leadership team to have a high degree of trust to let go. The response to this was overwhelming, and discretionary effort improved at all levels as a consequence.

The SHINE recognition scheme was welcomed by all employees. It provided the organisation with a great way to recognise good behaviour. Managers were able to nominate employees for any of the SHINE components and application forms were available to download from the company's intranet site. The applications went to the employee forum, who would consider and review the nominations in the first instance, sending a shortlist to the leadership team on a quarterly basis.

Those who made the shortlist would receive public recognition through a mention in the company newsletter and on specially created SHINE noticeboards. Quarterly award winners would go forward to an annual SHINE awards dinner hosted by the company.

Through the implementation of the SHINE initiatives, this organisation was able to not only maintain, but also enhance its position within the Best Companies list.

Raise Awareness – Employee engagement & recognition summary

Having an engaged workforce can pay dividends, and it's especially important when you're building an inclusive workplace culture. Creating a place where people come to work to give their best every day and are motivated to contribute to the organisation's success has got to be a win/win for both employee and employer.

Raise Awareness – Company Values

A value is a belief that guides your company choices and actions. It will help shape your workplace through recruitment and retention strategies, bring together your employees through engagement, and define the way you treat your customers, shareholders and stakeholders.

Organisations can spend thousands on either internal man hours or external consultants to help shape company values. However, if you want to get buy in from your employees, then involve them in the creation of your company values. This will enable everyone to understand what's required of them.

Communication is key. Share your company values and explain what they mean to the business and the staff, ensuring they are written in such a way that makes them easy to understand for everyone. Engage with staff and reinforce your core values frequently through written, spoken or visual communication. Just as importantly, ensure senior management lead by example.

It was important for me to set out my company values when I first launched my Jungle consultancy practice in 2008. Our values are:

– To be passionate about improvement

– To inspire people

– To unleash talent and creativity

– To think outside the box and be different

– To be innovative and have fun

These values are as relevant today as they were in 2008, but how my team and I apply them has changed. Our focus is to make a sustainable and impactful difference in everything that we do. We therefore align our business strategy with two of the United Nations Sustainable Development Global Goals:

– Global Goal number 5: gender equality

– Global Goal number 2: zero hunger

As such, we're proud ambassadors of the Hunger Project: a global charity dedicated to ending hunger by

2030. Our alignment with the Hunger Project enables us to demonstrate our commitment to helping others through financial support. In turn, the Hunger Project empowers, educates and trains women in developing countries, delivering change through people to end hunger in a sustainable way.

It's now up to us to build a better future for everyone. I would urge you to consider how you can align your company values with one of the United Nations Global Goals. Find out more at www.globalgoals.org

Defining your company values

A lot of work will go into crafting your business strategy and mission statement. Your core values form the identity of your company and workplace culture. You need them to show what differentiates your organisation from others.

As your organisation grows and matures, your company values may change, too. This is a good thing. Your core values reflect your actual values and how your organisation operates.

 Take a moment and consider these examples of company values. Do your values include any of these elements? If so, how are they showing up in your business. If your values don't reflect any of these elements, what could you do?

Sustainability and environmental matters. This can be how you manage things such as recycling and your approach to anything from single use water bottles through to printing, the packaging of your products or the energy you use within your business etc.

Innovation and excellence. This could be through research and development, enabling breakthroughs in technology resulting in new products or services. Such breakthroughs may positively impact on the lives of others.

If you place excellence at the centre of what you do, as opposed to pure profit, and ensure that whatever you design is of the highest quality, then you are not only giving the greatest value, but also making the biggest difference.

Placing people at the centre. A core value that sits well with inclusion could be 'openness, honesty, courage, respect, diversity and balance'. Believe it or not, this is Disney's corporate culture value for its team members. It places its people at the heart of everything it does, and encourages staff to share its values with each other and when interacting with customers. Disney expects its values to permeate the organisation, and by spelling this out to every team member at the induction stage, it clarifies what it expects from its staff.

Building communities. This is important when you're bringing about a cultural change, particularly one that is inclusive and embraces diversity. Your company can make a commitment to understanding the community in which it operates. Take a look around you – tune into the surrounding socio-economic environment.

By making a commitment to building strong communities, you could look for ways to fund programmes in local deprived areas. This may be through sporting activities, sponsoring school education programmes, enabling staff members to participate in mentoring or volunteering schemes, or raising funds through activities that bring teams together.

Raise awareness – Company values summary

Setting clear company values and making them visible can be advantageous to your employees and customers, influencing your brand and reputation as they define what your company stands for.

 Here are some top tips:

- **Be clear on your company values.** Think about your personal values, involve your employees, and get clear on the purpose of your business.

- **Consistently follow your company values.** Don't water them down or pick and choose when you use them. Apply them consistently in all activities, such as hiring new employees and decision making.

- **Weave your company values into everything you do.** This includes your operating practices, policies, procedures, and how you engage with employees and customers.

- **Share them with pride.** Don't hide your company values away – share them widely with your employees, on your company website, and with customers. Your company values make you uniquely you. They represent who and what you stand for. Great company values will help to attract and retain the best talent – you'll be seen as an employer of choice.

Your company values cannot be standalone. They cannot just be written down, they must live and breathe within your organisation. They will form part of your company's identity. They will set out your principles, beliefs and philosophies, and will enable your employees and your customers, stakeholders and shareholders to know who you are and what you stand for.[25]

---

25 www.forbes.com/sites/mikekappel/2018/07/25/how-to-create-a-company-culture-that-embodies-your-core-values/#1f381e083cc6

Raise Awareness – Summary And Checklist

Creating an inclusive workplace culture is important, so you need to raise awareness of not only why it's important, but also the 'what's in it for me?' element.

When something is different, we can often feel unsure. Even though many individuals agree it's the right thing to do to create inclusive workplace cultures, in truth they may not fully understand what this means.

In this section, I have given you some key areas to focus on which will help you raise awareness of inclusion and diversity. I have also highlighted that whatever initiatives you chose to implement, they should not be done in isolation. Align them as much as possible with your 'business as usual' activities.

Creating an inclusive culture is not just the role of HR; it's the role of everyone. In this section, I have therefore highlighted the importance of helping everyone to understand their role and contribution.

Let's recap on how you can raise awareness within your organisation.

Raise awareness checklist

- **Incredible leaders**

    ☐ Are your leaders aware of their impact?

    ☐ Do you use psychometric and personality profiling tools as a reference point to increase personal awareness?

    ☐ Do your leaders positively demonstrate empathy for others?

    ☐ Do they have an unquenchable thirst for learning?

    ☐ Do they recognise the value that a diverse workforce brings and the different ideas that it generates?

    ☐ Are they willing to show their vulnerability, reaching out for help to fill knowledge gaps, allowing others to step into their brilliance?

    ☐ Do they champion inclusion and diversity?

☐ Are they trusted and credible, showing genuine interest in others, honouring their commitment, and taking time to build solid relationships?

☐ Are they available for individuals as well as teams?

☐ Do they set time aside to listen to what employees have to say, giving them their undivided attention?

☐ Do they understand the polarities of leadership and perform the continual balancing act with courage and conviction?

- **Unconscious bias**

☐ Do you understand what unconscious bias is and the impact it has on decision making?

☐ Do you tune in to the biases of your colleagues within an organisation, helping them to understand the impact these have on others?

☐ Are you aware of the difference between prejudice and discrimination?

☐ Do you enable open conversations to take place so that people can truly understand what life is like within your organisation?

☐ Are you aware of other senses that can be used to promote decision making?

☐ Do you enable individuals to work alongside a diverse range of people as equals?

☐ Do you educate people around stereotypes?

☐ Do you make unconscious bias training voluntary?

☐ Do you provide networks/safe spaces for people to share experiences?

☐ Do you reach out to communities and become part of the community?

☐ Do you recognise challenges faced by minority groups within your organisation and work with them to build creative solutions?

☐ Have you set up a diversity council and forum?

☐ Have you made diversity and inclusion the responsibility of all employees?

– **Health and wellbeing**

☐ Do you enable open conversations to take place within your organisation around health and wellbeing?

☐ Do you provide clarity around the use of technology, respecting people's need to have time away from the work environment?

☐ Do you have systems and processes in place to support individuals who may need assistance managing stress, anxiety or mental health issues?

☐ Do you have, or have you considered implementing an employee assistance programme?

☐ Do you promote healthy eating within the workplace?

☐ Do you offer transparent rules, systems, and policies and procedures that create a respectful workplace? An environment free from bullying, harassment, and sexual harassment? Do these policies clearly set out your approach to dealing with any allegations, should they arise, and enabling your workforce to feel respected and courteous towards each other?

– **Healthcare**

☐ Have you considered the healthcare provision you offer as part of your remuneration package?

☐ Do you encourage all of your employees to participate in physical activity, promoting the benefits of increasing health and wellbeing?

☐ Have you extended your health and wellbeing policies and tied these into other family-friendly policies, enabling individuals to feel supported when their family situations change?

- **Employee engagement**

  ☐ Do you have an employee engagement plan in place?

  ☐ Have you communicated your plan so that it's widely understood within your business?

  ☐ Have you made your leaders accountable and fully committed to the delivery of a great place to work?

  ☐ Have you explored how the United Nations Global Goals can align with your organisation's vision to create a better world for everyone?

  ☐ Do you promote work-life balance, having the right policies in place?

  ☐ Do you regularly gather employee feedback?

  ☐ Do you have an employee recognition scheme in place?

- **Company values**

  ☐ Have you revisited your company values and ensured that they are representative of who you are?

  ☐ Have you shared your company values widely with your workforce?

☐ Have you aligned your company values, where possible, with a bigger purpose, such as the United Nations Global Goals, enabling everyone to build a better future?

☐ Did you involve your employees in the creating of the company values?

☐ Do your employees know and understand your values?

☐ Do you consistently follow your company values?

☐ Do you weave your company values into everything that you do?

Raising awareness about an inclusive workplace culture isn't just one or two activities; as you can see from this section, it's multifaceted. The approaches I have outlined throughout 'Raise Awareness' will enable you to build a sustainably inclusive workplace culture that will encourage your employees to be engaged and motivated to want to deliver their best.

SECTION 3

INSPIRE AND INVOLVE

Inspire And Involve – Introduction

This is an important phase of the tribe5 Diversity & Inclusion methodology, so it needs to form an integral part of your inclusion plan – a plan which should be transformative in terms of both behavioural and structural change.

In this section, we explore:

- **Male advocacy, ambassadors and allies** – the importance of male business leaders continuing to be great at what they do while becoming enablers for others, allowing a shift in our workplace to take place.

- **Role models** – the importance of having visible, real-life, relatable role models and creating a platform for these role models to shine through, enabling others to resonate with them. It's as much what they say as what they do that has an impact on others.

– **Mentoring** – offers great opportunities for both the mentor and the mentee. Mentoring programmes that inspire and involve people can enhance diversity and reinforce inclusive behaviours.

– **Stretch assignments or projects** – these are opportunities for individuals to broaden their experience, gaining confidence in other areas of the business to prepare themselves for career progression.

These activities are key components of enabling your whole workforce to feel involved in your inclusion journey. They will inspire others to recognise their unique differences and become ambassadors of the change you want to see.

Are you ready to inspire others? Let's begin.

Inspire And Involve – Male Advocacy

Male advocacy is a hugely important component in the drive to shape an inclusive workplace culture.

The reality is it's currently a man's world. It isn't 'men's fault'. It's no-one's 'fault'; it's a reflection of a society which might have been right for times gone by, but doesn't reflect our societal needs of today. Thankfully, society is evolving over the years.

The societal change is creating a movement spearheaded by women and advocated by men. This movement must be kept in the spotlight and placed high on leadership agendas, otherwise we will never make progress. We need momentum for various reasons, many of which I share in this book. This momentum for me is very much about inclusion rather than exclusion, yet it's causing concern for some.

Here's an example of what I mean.

CASE STUDY – THROUGH MALE EYES

I attended a forum around the gender pay gap. There was an audience of 200, and of that 200, only two were men.

In one regard, it was great. In another, the speakers (the majority of whom were women) were talking to an already converted audience. I firmly believe that we need these conversations to take place, but we need men to want and feel able to come along and participate.

Both the men in the audience stood up to speak. One, a senior leader of a large public sector organisation, made a poignant statement:

'In truth, I am scared about what all of this means for me as a senior leader. As we move further up the organisation, senior leadership roles become fewer. And if we are consciously saying they need to be filled by a certain gender, then what does that mean for me?'

This statement provoked emotional responses from some members of the audience. But my interpretation was 'I'm worried about what this means, don't exclude us, take us with you.'

The second point was made by the other man.
He stood up and said, 'I will be really honest with you. I too wish to have all of the flexible working arrangements that women are advocating. I have a family, but I don't see them during the week. I leave for work on a Sunday night. I don't get home until late on a Friday. I want to play an active part in my children's lives and be involved in their schooling, not just sign the cheque every term. However, I know that if I make requests for any sort for flexible working or show I'm not present in the office, it will affect my career.'

At that point, responses from the audience included, *'Well, now you know what we feel like.'* This, however, wasn't the point I believe he was trying to make. In actual fact, the movement towards creating an inclusive workplace culture is of equal importance to men as it is for women.

In his book *Confessions of a Working Father*, Brian Ballantyne captures these sentiments as he insightfully reflects upon his personal journey as a working father. Brian shares with candour and humour the challenges he faced, recognising the collaborative strength which is generated through the balance of equality within not only his home life, but also through his professional career.

The change I'm advocating through the tribe5 Diversity & Inclusion methodology isn't just about improving the lives of one gender, but all genders. Closing the gap is not a gender or ethnicity battle. Inclusion is for everybody's benefit; it's about everybody, not a divide.

Ambassadors, advocates and allies

To achieve continued momentum, we need male role models. Currently within the corporate environment, there is a significant proportion of (typically white) males operating in boardrooms and holding senior leadership positions. They have no need to apologise for this, but they do need to acknowledge that it's not reflective of our society and give consideration to the contributions they can make in reshaping the landscape within organisations.

One way in which we can achieve this is for our male counterparts to step forward and become ambassadors, advocates and allies. But what does this mean?

An ally is anyone who is interested in advocating for the rights of others. Someone willing to support and improve the outcomes for those in a minority within the workplace. Here are four key areas male ambassadors and advocates can focus on which will LEAD to allyship.

Look and listen – male ambassadors, advocates and allies can tune in to what they see and hear around them, for example what are the demographics in meetings or project groups? Is it always the same familiar faces? Does everyone have equal airtime in meetings?

Educate – Stephen Covey talks about *'Seek first to understand, then to be understood'*. A strength of an ally is their desire to understand different perspectives, so they proactively seek to educate themselves. They will reach out to minority groups and be unafraid to explore and ask.

Action – a good ally shows their support through their actions, such as confronting unacceptable behaviour or comments, or noticing and acting upon a lack of representation in the room. They show up and won't stand in the shadows.

Determination – allies have a thirst for learning. They are open to new ideas. They recognise that they can't always be right, in charge or have the best idea, understanding that it's better to listen to others and enable their advancement as this helps them to grow too.

We need to shift our boardrooms' demographics so that they become more diverse, not just in relation to gender (which the government has set voluntary targets against), but also in terms of other protected characteristics such as race, faith, disability and sexual orientation. Boardrooms need to become more representative of the customer base they serve.

Inspire and involve – Male advocacy summary

I firmly believe that we need our male business leaders to continue to be great at what they do, but we also need them to become ambassadors, advocates and allies. To LEAD. To be advocates of inclusion and recognise that this can be achieved through diversity. To support minority groups around them, whether it be race, gender, age, disability, faith, sexual orientation, with the ultimate aim of recognising and valuing the talent which is in front of them every day. To enable individuals to become the best version of themselves.

In the words of Mahatma Gandhi, *'Be the change you want to see in the world'*.

Inspire And Involve – Role Models

Daniel Priestley, entrepreneur and bestselling author, talks about how *'environment dictates performance'*. And that includes surrounding yourself with inspiring role models.

Research shows that boys tend to reference sport stars as role models and will often have much more awareness of business icons. Because of a lack of female corporate role models, typically these business icons are male. Young girls tend to look to television, magazines, pop stars and reality TV for their inspirational role models. And while female celebrities can be inspirational – you only have to look at Meghan Markle – they can also skew our vision of reality.

However, television producers are becoming increasingly in tune with society, and this is starting to be reflected in what we see on our TV screens daily. Women report on and read the news, present children's programmes, and even regenerate as Dr Who.

When you're creating your inclusive workplace culture, it's important to celebrate the accessible role models who are in front of you each and every day. Enable them to articulate their desires, dreams, hopes, fears and challenges to allow others to resonate with them in some way. They may spark something inside other people that inspires them to believe in possibilities too.

Providing a platform for role models across all protected characteristics – race, disability, gender, sexual orientation – enables your workforce to see, recognise and value the diverse skills and expertise that others bring. It's important, however, to understand that not everyone believes or feels that they're a role model at all. They're just doing something that feels natural to them, something they're proud to do, and something that makes a difference.

Role models don't come in the form of a job title, or only appear at a certain tier within a hierarchy, although leaders do hold a privileged and influential position in an organisation. A role model can be a leader who has the ability to share their wisdom, knowledge and expertise to enable others. Bear in mind, though, that leaders can also assert their power and authority inappropriately to dull someone else's sparkle. This is something we will cover in the 'Stretch Assignments' chapter as it plays an important role in the 'Inspire and Involve' phase of creating an inclusive culture.

Build your role model platform

Recognising your own biases is important when you're creating your diversity and inclusion strategy. If you're not sure what your biases are, then go back and take a look at the *Raise Awareness – Unconscious Bias* chapter. Build your role model platform with sensitivity, respect and care. Shape a mechanism that facilitates opportunities for individuals who inspire others to come forward and provide a way for them to receive the appropriate recognition for the contribution that they make to the lives of others. Remember that recognition can take many forms. Some individuals welcome overt recognition, while others prefer a more subtle approach.

We will cover this in more detail in later chapters.

If at present your organisation lacks the diversity to be able to identify role models from across all the protected characteristics, I encourage you to reach out to networks and local communities. There you will see individuals who may not identify themselves as being inspirational role models to others, but once you engage with them, they are likely to be only too willing to share their stories. These stories may include challenges they've overcome or career paths they've followed to arrive at their current role.

Reaching out is also a great way to establish and strengthen external relationships, building your business brand in the local community. Others will see just how serious your organisation is about diversity and inclusion. This is something we expand upon in the *Embed* section of the tribe5 Diversity & Inclusion methodology.

Creating a platform for role models to shine can take many forms.

 Here are a few ways in which you can get started:

- Create an environment where individuals feel safe and supported to share something they are proud of, perhaps during a one-to-one meeting. Your role can be to encourage them to feel confident enough to share in team meetings.

- Shape a mechanism that facilitates opportunities for individuals who inspire others to come forwarded/be nominated.

- Hold 'inspire speaker' sessions on a regular basis, inviting someone from the organisation to share their career journey, the challenges they faced and their hopes for the future. These speaker slots should be made available to all employees so that they can put themselves forward or nominate someone else to host a talk. Make the sessions accessible to a wide audience, considering the best time of day to hold them.

- Use technology so that individuals can record short videos and upload them on to a diversity and inclusion platform for everyone to see.

- Produce communication materials that enable all employees to experience a day in the life of someone else.

- Invite guest speakers from other companies or from the local community to share the work they are doing or their personal story to inspire others.

Inspire and involve - Role model summary

Inspirational role models are around us every day. They could be people who have shown considerable strength and tenacity while battling with an illness or living with a disability. They could be a historical icon who changed society and made a difference in the world, or a scientist who created a cure for a life-threatening condition. Equally, a role model could be somebody who quietly does the thing that they're passionate about, day in, day out, seeking neither glory nor recognition, just wanting to make a difference.

In truth, most individuals are modest (although there are exceptions to the rule – I've worked with a few). By offering a platform/mechanism whereby your employees can hear, see and talk to different and diverse individuals, you provide them with vital education. Equally, hearing from someone they resonate with may spark something in employees which enables them to value the difference that they bring. It may ultimately inspire them to step into their brilliance and do something different.

Inspire And Involve – Mentoring

Coaching and mentoring – it's the same thing, right?

Wrong!

The terms coaching and mentoring are often used interchangeably within the workplace. Some managers believe they are coaching members of their team when in fact they are giving out instructions. Others believe they are mentoring someone by showing them how to do a task.

Individuals looking to progress in their careers and in need of some wise counsel may ask, 'Does it really matter because the distinction is so insignificant?' Yes, it matters. In this chapter, I will break down the subtle but vital distinction between coaching and mentoring. I will also help you to understand the important role that both can play in creating an inclusive workplace culture.

So, let me help to dispel some myths and try and provide some clarity around the differences between coaching and mentoring.

What is coaching?

- Coaching is a form of developmental support
- The coaching relationship is often short term, lasting only for as long as required
- The aim of coaching is usually task focused
- Coaching is about enabling someone to be their best
- Coaching is unlocking people's potential to maximise their own performance
- Unlike mentoring, coaching is not about advice
- A coach will usually work with a coachee for a specific purpose such as achieving a personal or professional goal, which may involve enhancing current skills or acquiring new skills

- At the commencement of the coaching programme, the coachee, the coach and often the sponsoring line manager agree goals
- Performance is measured against these goals to check that the coachee is making progress

Once the skills are successfully acquired the coach is no longer needed. There are many reasons why an individual may seek out or be identified as potentially benefiting from coaching. Perceptions around why individuals may benefit from working with a coach have, thankfully, changed over the past few years. Historically, coaching may have been viewed as a remedial sanction, a sort of punishment for poor performance. Yet conversely, if sportspeople want to excel, it's always been commonplace for them to work with a coach to improve their performance. Thankfully, the corporate world now takes a similarly positive view of coaching in the workplace and recognises the benefits it brings.

A requirement for coaching may arise as part of leadership development and be prompted by developmental feedback. Some individuals receive transitional coaching when they take on a new role or move into a different functional area. Organisations can also offer coaching during times of disruption, such as mergers, transitions and cultural changes, particularly when mindsets and beliefs have to alter.

Coaching provides a safe space for the coachee to be listened to and constructively challenged. The coach will often spring free thoughts and ideas from the coachees by asking powerful, non-judgemental yet probing questions, but the true power of coaching manifest outside the coaching session, ie in between sessions when the individual has had time to reflect and put some of their new skills into practice.

Coaching has many benefits, including facilitating a change in attitude and behaviour, which in turn can significantly improve the culture and motivation of your workforce. Coaching is typically offered by an external professional, although some companies operate internal coaching programmes. Establishing rapport between coach and coachee is vital when you're selecting a coach. They need to have mutual respect and trust, preserving the confidentiality of the coaching session, the only caveat being a professional obligation on the part of the coach to report something illegal or immoral.

What is mentoring?

Mentoring is a long-term relationship between two individuals. It's development driven, its purpose being to support the growth of an individual not only in their current job, but also for future roles.

Mentorship typically occurs when a more experienced or knowledgeable person guides a less experienced or knowledgeable person. A mentor will freely share their experiences, the mistakes as well as the successes.

'Mentoring involves primarily listening with empathy, sharing experience (usually mutually), professional friendship, developing insight through reflection, being a sounding board, encouraging.'
— David Clutterbuck

A mentor understands their role is to be dependable, engaged and authentic. They will role model behaviours. Both the mentor and the mentee can learn about one another and build a climate of trust, creating an environment in which the mentee feels secure in sharing the real issues that are impacting on his or her success.

Reverse mentoring

As mentorship is a learning and development partnership based on knowledge and experience, reverse mentoring can be equally impactful. Here a senior individual may be mentored by someone in a more junior position or from an underrepresented group. This relationship not only enables the sharing of business experience, but allows a mutual transfer of knowledge to take place.

This level of sharing can enhance business performance, enabling a company to gain a competitive advantage.

Mentoring as part of talent planning

Extensive research shows that women will only put themselves forward for jobs or career advancement when they believe that they possess all the skills and experience required to fulfil the job. This can create a barrier to women's advancement, particularly if there are limited opportunities for them to gain the additional experience they believe they need to obtain. When you offer mentoring as part of your company's talent and succession planning strategy, you provide an opportunity for women to be supported. Mentoring can build confidence and accelerate career advancements, and the mentor can also gain valuable insight through the mentoring relationship.

Here's an example of how.

CASE STUDY - THE POWER OF MENTORING

A manufacturing organisation introduced a mentorship scheme across its senior leadership team. The initiative was part of its talent strategy with a specific focus on strengthening the female talent pipeline.

The company fully scoped out the scheme, clearly defining mentoring boundaries, roles and responsibilities. It designed and implemented codes of conduct, which included the importance of confidentiality. These steps enabled those who participated in the programme to feel safe and supported.

A matching process took place whereby female members of the senior leadership team were matched with their male counterparts. However, it quickly became apparent that there were significantly more males than females. This led the organisation to widen the scope of its mentoring programme to include women who held roles within the two tiers below executive level.

The company initially offered the mentorship scheme on a pilot basis, seeking feedback from the individuals involved in the programme. This feedback raised awareness around the challenges faced by female leaders, particularly those returning to the workplace after maternity leave.

Overall, the organisation recognised the benefits of operating a mentoring scheme and looked to extend the scope of the programme more widely within the business.

If you don't yet have a mentoring scheme within your organisation, now is a great time to start. Ensuring that it is set up properly is really important, so here are some top tips.

 ## Top tips on creating a mentoring scheme

Purpose. When you're setting up a mentoring scheme, be clear from the outset exactly what you're looking to achieve. Consider:

- How does your mentoring programme tie in to other development support offered by your organisation?

- Is your mentoring programme part of your talent planning strategy?

- Is it a talent retention mechanism?

- What other outcomes are you looking to achieve through the mentoring programme?

Scope. The next step is to be clear on who will be involved in the mentoring programme. Is the programme open to all employees or do you want to limit the scope to particular levels within your organisation? Will you offer mentoring to new employees as part of their induction programme, or will you offer it by way of a talent planning mechanism? Whatever the route you choose, ensure that it is inclusive and equitable.

Remember, mentoring is about the sharing of experience, so widen the scope as far as possible to maximise its benefit.

Programme promotion. Clearly promote the mentoring scheme to enable everyone to fully understand what it is and who it's open to. Remember, not everyone who would benefit from mentoring will proactively put themselves forward, but the more you promote the scheme and share success stories, the more people will understand how beneficial mentoring can be (for both the mentor and the mentee) and the more successful the scheme will become.

 When promoting the scheme, you should also consider:

– Communicating the purpose of the programme

– Sharing details of who is eligible to participate

– Providing information about how often the scheme is open to new participants

– Being clear on how mentor and mentees can apply to join the scheme

– Clearly setting out the benefits to both the mentor and mentee

– Sharing success stories – celebrating where it worked well

Selecting your mentors. Next, you will need to identify who will become a mentor. It's important to establish as an organisation whether your first approach will be to accept anyone willing to volunteer as a mentor, or whether you wish to formalise the process and invite individuals to apply. There's merit in both approaches, but ensure that those who volunteer are not the same people who always step up for other opportunities. Provide a platform for mentors to be selected as broadly as possible, remembering to encourage those who may not readily put themselves forward or see themselves as a mentor.

A mentor is somebody who will role model congruent behaviours. They must be willing to share their experience and knowledge freely as the mentoring relationship provides an opportunity for both parties to learn extensively from each other and the life journeys they have travelled.

It's important to offer training to those who step forward to become mentors. This will ensure that they are set up for success and are suitably equipped to carry out the role.

Matching. The next stage is to match the mentees with an appropriate mentor.

The purpose of mentorship is, of course, to enable the sharing of knowledge and experience between the parties. However, it's equally important to establish rapport between the individuals. Mentorship is about personal growth and development, so a positive relationship is key.

As part of the scoping programme, your organisation will have established the purpose of the mentoring relationship and set out broadly how it will work. Once the matching process has taken place, it's important for both parties to mutually agree how the mentoring relationship will work.

 Areas to consider include:

- The frequency of the mentoring sessions. Too often can impact on other commitments, but infrequent mentoring sessions can negatively affect the overall effectiveness of the programme.

- What issues are appropriate to raise within the mentoring session, and what should be raised through other support programmes provided by the company?

- Where mentoring sessions will take place. This will be agreed between the parties within the parameters defined by the programme rules. Some individuals prefer mentoring sessions to take place within the office environment, others prefer a more relaxed environment, choosing to meet in an off-site venue.

- How technology can aid flexibility around when and where mentoring sessions take place. Technology can provide a positive solution to those who require more flexible working patterns, but may be matched with someone who carries out extensive travelling.

- Records/notes made during the mentoring relationship. These should be in accordance with the UK GDPR regulations to preserve confidentiality.

Accountability. Mentoring is about movement as it provides a platform for growth and development. The mentor will expect the mentee to update on the progress they've made and the challenges they've faced. A mentor will hold the mentee to account, so it's important to highlight the accountability element of mentoring. We all lead busy lives, but the mentee needs to recognise the importance of completing all of the tasks they agree to complete.

Pilot the programme. If you're new to operating a mentoring programme, it's sensible to run a pilot. This will enable the organisation to establish the programme's effectiveness and make any changes to the mentoring scheme prior to rolling it out widely within the business. The pilot could involve a specific department or group of individuals.

Celebrating success. It's important to celebrate the successes which a mentoring scheme can bring. This could include sharing success stories via newsletters or other internal communication channels, showcasing the benefits that mentoring has offered to both mentor and mentee. This may encourage individuals with less confidence to step forward and participate in the scheme, and it is a great way of recognising both parties, too.

Keeping up to date. Mentors should continue to receive support, guidance and development themselves. This can take the form of supervision sessions through action learning sets. These supervision sessions may include the sharing of experiences and provide an opportunity for best practice training.

Inspire and involve – Mentoring summary

Having an internal mentoring programme brings both merits and challenges. The merits are that it can be implemented within an organisation for little to no cost, sharing company knowledge and expertise widely within the business. Both the mentor and mentee experience personal development and growth through the process. However, limited diversity within your organisation significantly reduces the opportunity to learn from the experiences of those of a different gender, age, sexual orientation or faith, or living with a disability.

If necessary, extend the reach of your mentoring programme to include external mentors to provide greater learning opportunities. You may also wish to collaborate with external companies that offer mentoring programmes, matching mentees and mentors within your business with those from different companies. By reaching outside your organisation for mentorship, you will widen the learning opportunities and experience the true benefits that a mentoring programme can bring.

Inspire And Involve – Development/Stretch Opportunities

It's not always possible to provide promotional opportunities for everyone – I get that. Sometimes the organisation's structure prevents it, or budgetary constraints mean that there's a lack of funding. And when promotional opportunities do arise, men are much more likely than women to step forward, regardless of whether they possess all the requisite skills, confident that they can learn as they go along. Women, on the other hand, tend to wait until they have 100% of the necessary role requirements. Only then do they feel confident that they have the capability as well as the qualifications to do the job.

Stretch assignments therefore need to be part of any organisation's inclusive strategy. Let me explain why.

What are stretch assignments?

Stretch assignments are opportunities for individuals to take on additional projects or secondments. Giving someone a task which is outside of their comfort zone can expand their knowledge, build their confidence, and prepare them for career progression. For the individual, stretch assignments provide a great opportunity to experience a new challenge at low risk. This can motivate them, enhance their skills and raise their internal and external profile.

Stretch assignments are a win-win for organisations as they develop capabilities which the business can draw upon for special projects or to cover absences, whether planned or not. They are a great way to tap in to leadership talent and can avoid any sticky floor or glass ceiling situations.

Stretch assignments come in all shapes and sizes, and can be short or long term. They are typically done in addition to normal job tasks, enhancing an individual's skill set and often, giving an individual exposure to different parts of the business and creating multi-disciplinary working environments.

 Some examples which you might wish to consider include:

- Organising an event or exhibition
- Joining a project team to manage a new project or give a fresh perspective to one that's ongoing
- Writing a proposal – this could be an internal business case or an external proposal for a client
- Starting or leading an internal group or becoming an advocate or mentor
- Taking the role of chair at internal meetings

Stretch assignments say to employees, 'There's a project that's come up and I think your skillset really lends itself to being involved in it', or 'We've had some discussions about you wanting to improve your business acumen; this will be a great opportunity for you to be part of a project team', or 'You've previously talked about wanting to develop your leadership skills so I'd like you to chair our team meetings.'

While some stretch opportunities might seem simple or insignificant, for those who wouldn't ordinarily step up to these opportunities, the stretch can be huge. But breakthroughs often happen when we are so far out of our comfort zones that we surprise ourselves.

Line manager role

Line managers play a vital role in making stretch opportunities happen. They need to be in step with their team, constantly looking for ways to develop all members and enable them to grow. An inclusive leader does not just favour individuals who look, think and sound like they do, only offering those individuals opportunities. An inclusive leader will understand the value that a diverse team brings and will seek opportunities to offer personal development to everyone.

For stretch assignments to work, line managers also need to learn to let go. I've experienced it when a manager doesn't involve their staff in opportunities because they want to keep all the opportunities for themselves (particularly the high-profile ones). They hold their team back because they're frightened others might perform better than them. Their team members might be the ones to come up with a winning idea, or offer a totally different perspective which leads to a breakthrough but they take the credit for themselves.

This is not the behaviour of a great leader and will not build an inclusive culture.

Getting started

If you don't already offer stretch assignments in your inclusion strategy, now is a great time to do so. Link this in to other strategies such as talent planning, recognition, employee engagement and performance review processes. If somebody wants to stretch, grow and develop, consider what opportunities you need to give them to build their confidence. It may be that they need to find their voice to speak out in meetings, so you could offer them the opportunity to chair the weekly team meetings. For some people, that would be quite a daunting experience, but it's a great opportunity in a safe environment.

Whatever stretch assignments you offer, it's important that you present them in such a way that the individual understands and recognises their benefits. The last thing you want is for someone to believe they're having more things added to their already busy workload and feel aggrieved because they're not being paid for doing these extra things. Communication between the line manager and the employee needs to be open, honest and two-way. The employee needs to know what the opportunity is and why you are inviting them to take part so they can feel excited by it (while also recognising that they may also feel somewhat daunted).

Inspire and involve – Development/ stretch opportunities summary

When you're creating an inclusive culture, make sure stretch assignments form part of its normal operating practice to ensure everyone in your organisation gets the opportunities to develop their skills and confidence. Offer stretch assignments widely and celebrate their successes.

Inspire And Involve –
Summary And Checklist

An inclusive workplace culture is not something that one individual can achieve; it is something that is felt/experienced by all. By undertaking activities which involve everyone and inspire them to recognise their unique differences, you will accelerate your inclusion journey.

Let's recap on some of the areas we've covered in this section.

To continue with the momentum in terms of increasing the presence of underrepresented groups in the workplace, we need male ambassadors, advocates and allies who will stand up for the rights of others, support those who are a minority and be willing to LEAD:

- Look and listen –tune in to what they see around them

- Educate – have a thirst for knowledge, proactively seeking the views and opinions of others

- Action – show their support through actions

- Determination – ambassadors and allies will listen to others and enable advancements

We absolutely need male leaders to continue to be great at what they do. We need them to enable and support others to be the best version of themselves. We need to surround ourselves with inspiring role models. These, however, can take many forms. It's not always celebrities and superstars or top performers who display inclusive behaviours; a role model can be anyone quietly achieving excellence on a daily basis.

Implementing mentoring schemes at all levels within your organisation is a great way to share knowledge and expertise, increasing awareness of differing views and perspectives. You can also ensure that you make developmental stretch opportunities/project assignments widely available to all employees to increase confidence and broaden experience.

Inspire and involve checklist

– **Male advocacy**

☐ Do you have male advocates and ambassadors within your organisation?

☐ Do they role model behaviours, supporting others and providing them with opportunities?

☐ Do you proactively encourage your male colleagues to take their full entitlement of family-friendly arrangements?

☐ Do your male ambassadors seek out opportunities to understand different perspectives from underrepresented groups?

☐ Do your ambassadors support and act when they see behaviour which is incongruent with that of an inclusive company?

☐ Do they value the talent in front of them?

– **Role models**

☐ Do you enable others to see, recognise and value the diverse skills and expertise that they have?

☐ Do you reach out to your local communities, developing relationships and networks, enabling role models to come into your organisation and share experiences which may inspire others?

☐ Do you provide opportunities every day for employees to share things that they are proud of during meetings or one-to-one sessions?

☐ Do you utilise technology to share success stories with all employees?

☐ Do you produce communication materials that enable all employees to experience a day in the life of someone else?

– **Mentoring**

☐ Does your organisation understand the difference between coaching and mentoring?

☐ Is mentoring available within your organisation?

☐ Do you offer mentoring to all employees within your business?

☐ Do you offer reverse mentoring?

☐ Are you clear about the purpose of a mentoring scheme?

☐ Are you inclusive when you select your mentors?

☐ How do you ensure your mentors and mentees are matched appropriately?

☐ How do you celebrate the success of a mentoring programme?

☐ How do you ensure that your mentors are suitably equipped and regularly developed as part of their mentoring role?

☐ Do you extend your mentoring programme to individuals outside your organisation?

☐ Do you offer your mentees to other organisations so that they can receive industry-wide mentoring?

☐ Does your senior leadership team proactively mentor those in underrepresented groups?

– **Stretch opportunities**

☐ Do your managers regularly identify stretch opportunities?

☐ Are these opportunities available for all employees?

☐ Do you ask members of your team to organise an event or exhibition?

☐ Have you invited people from different departments or levels to join a project team?

☐ Have you asked for wider views and opinions when writing business proposals or internal business cases?

☐ Have you asked employees to set up an internal inclusion group?

☐ Have you asked employees to become an advocate or mentor?

☐ Do you rotate the chair at team meetings?

☐ Are your managers willing to let go of tasks in order to facilitate successful stretch opportunities?

☐ Do you celebrate the success of individuals once they have participated in stretch opportunities?

The above are suggestions for how you can inspire and involve others. It's not a one-size-fits-all and you may even be doing some things I've not listed here. What's important is that when employees are included, they will feel a connection with your organisation. They will feel like they belong, and as a result, they'll want to play an active role in its success.

SECTION 4

BUILD FOR THE FUTURE

Build For The Future – Introduction

Building for the future is the degree to which your business is fit for purpose, ensuring that you have the right structures and talent in place for success. Your inclusion and diversity strategy plays an integral part in this and should be closely aligned with your business strategy.

In this section, I will explore the importance of breaking with tradition and building a culture which inspires the next generation. I also guide you through how to place your people at the heart of your business.

- **Business continuity** – for your business to look at the continuity of its people and consider the risk management associated with a loss of talent.

- **Talent planning** – how developing a talent map, which is regularly calibrated, can help you to successfully deliver against your business plan as well as ensure that you're attracting the best talent from the widest and most diverse pool.

- **Diversity and inclusion networks** – the importance of diversity and inclusion forums and networks to enable open conversations, share experiences, and continue to build inclusive work environments for the future.

- **Returnships** – individuals can take a period of time away from the workplace for a number of reasons, whether it be due to raising a family, sickness or redundancy. Any period of absence can significantly dent the confidence of even the most rounded and well-experienced professionals, and the prospect of returning to work can feel daunting. A returnship programme can offer great opportunities to tap into a rich pool of talent, reaching out to those individuals who might otherwise struggle to get a foot back on the career ladder. These individuals offer experience and a different perspective.

– **Training and development** – ensuring that your managers are set up for success and equipped with all the management and leadership tools and techniques to be as proficient as possible.

– **Leadership education** – it's important that leaders understand their impact on others and how their unconscious bias may influence the decisions that they make.

Building for the future and putting people at the heart of everything you do will enable your organisation to transition towards an inclusive culture. Let's take a look at the steps you can take.

Build For The Future – Business Continuity

I'm not a glass half empty sort of person, but it's important to consider how you would manage your operating practices should something unexpected occur.

Many organisations will have a business continuity or disaster recovery plan in place. A business continuity plan is a working document which will help an organisation to mitigate disruptions when it's not able to operate due to an emergency or disaster. By having a business continuity plan, your organisation will be able to return to its daily operations as quickly as possible. Key staff are typically assigned specific responsibilities and know what is expected of them at such times, which means customer disruption and loss of revenue are kept to a minimum.

A disaster recovery plan is a set of procedures which everyone within an organisation follows in the event of a disaster, be it natural, environmental or man-made. When creating your plan, you may need to consider such factors as:

– What to do in the event of something happening to the office building or factory premises

– What would happen if there was an IT system failure?

– What would happen if there was a power outage?

– How would you deal with a cyber-attack or mechanical breakdown?

Considering these factors is really important for ensuring the smooth and effective operation of your organisation, but what does business continuity and disaster recovery have to do with creating an inclusive workplace culture, you might well ask? Well, sadly many organisations fail to consider their people when creating their business continuity or disaster recovery plans. Yet it's the people who are the organisations' greatest assets.

Let me give you some examples of why you should consider your people within your business continuity and disaster recovery plan, and the potential implications if you fail to do so.

CASE STUDY – TRAVEL PLANNING

Each year, a leading travel company would take its executive board and senior leadership team away to an off-site leadership conference. While this was a truly wonderful opportunity for the leadership team to get together, usually in a beautiful location, it also meant extensive travel planning.

To comply with the disaster recovery plan, executive board members were not permitted to travel together. Senior leaders were not permitted to travel with either the executive team or their team members, and so on. This measure was put in place to safeguard the business should an unfortunate accident occur, but it required precision planning to ensure that everyone was in the right place at the right time.

 Next time you organise an event such as an all-employee annual conference or a sales conference, consider the measures you need to put in place for travel planning. How do you safeguard key members of your executive board or personnel?

CASE STUDY – COMING INTO MONEY

I often hear people say, 'If I won the lottery, I'd go off travelling the world.' Well, this scenario unfolded for one organisation. It wasn't, however, as a result of a lottery syndicate win, but a key incentive plan the company had itself put in place, intending it as a mechanism to reward and retain senior leaders within the business.

The organisation had implemented the long-term incentive plan as part of its executive remuneration strategy. The business had performed well over several years and was on target to hit all of the projected financial returns. This was great news and the incentive scheme had achieved its aim. However, what the company hadn't anticipated was that for some individuals, the financial incentive was the equivalent of a lottery win. A number of key executives upon receiving their incentive chose to leave the business to travel the world.

 Finally, consider how you manage the continuity of your workforce, particularly when you have to ramp up staffing levels during periods of high demand, which may be seasonal.

CASE STUDY – SEASONAL WORKING

A service business recognised that it had reached maximum capacity within its call centre. Nevertheless, it needed to increase its workforce on a temporary basis to meet customer demands during the busy winter months.

As part of its business continuity plan, the organisation explored innovative ways in which it could meet its resourcing needs without expanding its call centre and decided to work with people who live in coastal communities. Typically, the winter months are quiet for coastal communities, and the company recognised that this population was a rich source of talent. It therefore set up a proactive recruitment campaign specifically in coastal areas.

The seasonal staff the company appointed as a result of this campaign were provided with the relevant technology, enabling them to handle the increased volume of calls that came in during the winter period from their homes. This innovative business continuity and talent planning tapped in to individuals who had great customer service experience, particularly as many had spent all summer being hosts to the hundreds of thousands of guests that came into their local community, all without the company having to expand its business premises to accommodate an increased headcount or compromise client service delivery.

Build for the future – Business continuity summary

People are, without a doubt, an organisation's most important asset, so never leave business continuity involving your people to chance.

Build For The Future – Talent Planning

Having a clear understanding of the talents, skills and behaviours of every employee in your company is vital, particularly in today's tough business climate.

Talent planning shouldn't be guesswork. It needs to be proactive as opposed to reactive, ie somebody's left and you now need to fill the position. Your approach needs to be aligned with your company's strategic focus. Essentially, look forward and horizon scan – where are you going? Then look back and identify the talent you already have within your workforce. Where are there gaps?

Introducing talent mapping into your organisation is just one means of ensuring success.

What is talent mapping?

Talent mapping will help you identify what the talent really looks like within your organisation. What skills and behaviours do you need to pursue the current business plan successfully?

Talent mapping charts every individual in a company according to their skills, competencies and capabilities. This information essentially forms the basis of your company talent map, which will enable you to analyse talent and potential. Where do your employees add value now and where can they deliver value in the future?

Some companies bring in external providers to help them set up talent management programmes. These experts bring an objective viewpoint, guiding companies through the entire process, teaching them how to spot talent, creating profiles for individuals, and setting up talent maps showing how individuals can be developed in a formal and structured way.

A talent map will help you focus on short-term goals without losing sight of the bigger picture. It will also help you with your long-range strategy and determine what talent you need to ensure future business success.

Talent should be developed

An individual's talents do not remain static. The world around is rapidly changing, and our knowledge and skills need to try and keep pace.

That's why continual learning is important. It's not always about going on a course; talent can be developed through knowledge sharing, shadowing, job swapping, mentoring and stretch assignments. One of the most important things is to ensure that your employees remain motivated and committed to doing the best job they can.

The role of the line manager

Line managers need to be coached on how to spot, nurture and develop talent. Include this as one of their performance objectives and empower them to invest in the time they need to ensure that their team realises career development is a major business priority. A talent map can enable your managers, at a glance, to see when employee development is needed, providing career progression opportunities in a timely manner.

Central to maximising the value of talent maps is your line managers' willingness to allow their people to progress within the organisation. They need to think about the business strategy as a whole. How much more valuable will their people be after their talent has been developed by working within other departments and moving out of their comfort zones?

Steps to better talent management

As with most business initiatives, there isn't one right way to 'do' talent management. Talent mapping is just one methodology.

 Here are some top tips to help you start implementing an effective talent management process.

- Identify the skills, knowledge and technical expertise you require to make the organisation succeed in the current economic climate. Make sure the requirements reflect the company's existing, emerging or desired culture.

- Find out the extent of your employees' talent and plot this on to a talent map. This will show what skills gaps can be filled by developing existing employees, and what skills need to be brought in from outside.

- Utilise your organisation's talent to maximum effect – be prepared to move your talent so that specific skills are located where they are needed most.

- Talent is dynamic and needs to be developed – use the talent map to see how you can add to individual talents and provide the appropriate tools to do this.

- Keep your talent map up to date – maintaining an accurate picture of what talent exists where within your organisation will enable you to adapt to changes in the business environment quickly and effectively.

- Ensure that your talent management strategy is linked to operational performance measures so you can clearly identify the 'value add'.

Here's a case study to showcase how talent planning can enable your organisation to become fit for the future.

CASE STUDY – TALENT CALIBRATION

Having conducted a review of its workforce demographics, a leading manufacturer recognised that it needed to focus its attention on its talent management strategy in order to become fit for the future. The company implemented an inclusive talent calibration system. This system meant that talent calibration sessions took place quarterly, whereas previously they had taken place annually.

The company ensured that the talent calibration system was aligned with the performance management system. This meant regular, but separate, performance and career conversations took place, the information from these sessions forming important data which was shared during the talent calibration review sessions.

The talent calibration process itself involved lots of touchpoints with different stakeholders. Employees assessed themselves. They also had an opportunity to seek feedback from colleagues should they wish. Team leaders were invited to share their feedback on the employees, as were the manager and department head. Having so many touchpoints enabled the company to gather wide views of everyone's performance.

This collective information was shared with the leadership team on a quarterly basis. Every member of the senior leadership team was involved in the quarterly calibration session, so they got to hear about the talent in each department. They used this information not only as part of their succession planning, but also to create stretch projects for individuals to help strengthen skills capability.

Build for the future – Talent planning summary

Talent mapping will help you identify what the talent really looks like within your organisation. You'll then understand what skills and behaviours you need to pursue the current business plan successfully.

It's important, however, not to pigeonhole employees. Talent planning isn't about how to keep people in the roles they're currently doing; it's about asking how to attract the best talent from a diverse pool. How do you grow your talent? How do you enable employees to move forward and shape their future?[26]

---

26 'Navigating through the talent management Jungle' by Teresa Boughey, August 2011

Build For The Future – Returnships

The term 'returnship' was first introduced (and trademarked) by Goldman Sachs in 2008 when the company commenced a ten-week paid programme specifically for individuals who'd had taken a substantial break from work.

Time away from work could be the result of raising a family, carer responsibilities, illness, or many other factors, but long-term absence often makes it difficult for an individual to reignite their career. The purpose of Goldman Sachs's returnship programme was to provide support, training to revitalise skillsets and work experience to high-potential individuals. During the returnship programme, these individuals were responsible for a specific project or task, and at the end, those selected were offered employment.

What are returnship programmes?

The concept of a returnship programme has gained popularity over the years with many companies now creating their own versions. Competition to participate in such programmes is fierce, often with an applicants-to-places ratio of at least ten to one.

Returnship programmes are not just aimed at women. Men also face challenges getting a foothold back on the career ladder when they have had long breaks from the workplace. However, with it being much more common for women to have time away from work, many organisations are now placing a particular emphasis on creating programmes that encourage women to return to work.

We know from research that when they reach childbearing age, women's careers progress at a much slower rate than those of their male counterparts. Many take time away from the workplace to achieve a better work-life balance and spend time with their families. I was one of those individuals. Following the birth of my second child (seventeen years after my first), I, like many other women, was faced with the dilemma of having to make a professional career choice. It was unsustainable for me to operate within the leadership role I'd attained; the demands of the role combined with the working hours meant that I had to make an 'either-or' decision.

I stepped off the corporate treadmill, and after a short break with my family, I chose to enter the world of entrepreneurship. This is so often the case for women who desire intellectual stimuli balanced with work flexibly to meet family needs.

A rich talent pool

When you're building an inclusive workplace culture, consider the benefits that a returnship programme can offer your organisation. There's a rich pool of talent with extensive experience and qualifications gained from former careers. Although not currently in the workplace on a day-to-day basis, these individuals have developed other equally important transferable talents such as financial planning, leadership, multitasking and organisational skills.

However, having any period of time away from the workplace, for whatever reason, can significantly dent the confidence of even the most rounded and experienced professional, so the prospect of returning to work can feel daunting. Returnship programmes are a means of equipping individuals with the skills and support they need to return confidently.

A long interview

While it's commendable that many organisations offer return to work schemes, a point raised by the All-Party Parliamentary Group for Women and Work focused on the genuineness of a job at the end of a programme. Some returnship schemes are offered to large groups of women, sometimes twenty to thirty individuals taking part. It's a wonderful networking opportunity, it builds camaraderie between the individuals and means the company can train a large group in a short time period. But, research has shown that the genuine offers of employment at the end of these schemes are often disproportionate to the number of individuals participating. The consequence is that it can often feel like a very long interview and selection process with a bitterly disappointing outcome.

Candidate confidence can be eroded further if there's no role available at the end of the returnship programme. It's therefore important when you're setting up such a programme that you ensure there are genuine positions on offer at the end of it.

Where it's not possible for you to offer the requisite number of positions at the end of returnship programmes within your own organisation, reach out and collaborate with other companies. Highlight the talent within your returnship programme while promoting job roles and opportunities with other firms. This will not only strengthen your own employer brand, but also increase the chances for those individuals returning to the workplace.

CASE STUDY – RETURNSHIPS FOR OLDER EMPLOYEES

Returnship programmes are primarily aimed at women, although many organisations are now extending the scope of such programmes to reflect other underrepresented groups. A leading DIY chain, for example, successfully introduced an age diversity programme and is now renowned for employing older people. The programme was initially launched in the northwest of England and subsequently rolled out to all of the chain's UK stores.

The objective for each store is to employ a workforce representative of the make-up of its local community. The chain recognised that older workers are an underused pool of talent and, through its pilot, proved the demonstrable business benefits in employing a diverse workforce.

Setting up a returnship programme

- Have an open mind – don't just look for candidates that fit the same mould as your current employees. Be open to a candidate's broad experience. Recognise that different industry sector experience may bring fresh perspectives.

- Consider the policies and procedures your organisation has in place. How do you handle flexible working requests? Does the architecture of the jobs within your structure enable job flexibility such as part-time working or job share?

- Planning is key – ensure the project or task the returner will be involved in is meaningful. The department they will be joining needs to have an on-boarding plan in place so that they can be welcomed and quickly orientated into the team.

- Educate managers on the benefits of the programme so that they fully understand the role they play in making it successful.

- Assign a buddy to each person taking part in the returnship programme. Having a single point of contact, someone familiar with the organisation to reach out to, can make a huge difference to someone settling back into the work environment. For the person being a buddy, this could satisfy a stretch/development opportunity.

- You can also offer mentoring to those taking part in a returnship programme, continuing this mentoring once they take up a permanent role. Offer them additional activities, too, such as spending time in other departments and lunchtime leadership conversations with members of the executive team.

- Integrate your leaver strategy with your returnship programme. Tracking who leaves your business, at what point and for what reason, will enable you to fully understand the talent that is exiting. You can then consider how you want to keep in touch with this population proactively while they are away so that they have the option to return to you in the future.

Finally, it's important to get feedback from those participating in the programme. How have they found the programme? Have they received sufficient support? What else could you do to make the programme more successful?

Build for the future - Returnships summary

Make returnship a key component of your organisation's inclusion strategy. If you're unable to offer a returnship programme within your own organisation, consider contacting businesses that are already hosting such schemes and explore your company requirements to establish if they match the focus of the programme. Alternatively, collaborate with other organisations to run combined schemes.

Surely, it's wasteful to let great talent pass you by. Implementing a returnship programme offers a great opportunity to tap into a rich pool of talent; to reach out to those individuals who might otherwise struggle to get a foot back on the career ladder. Individuals who will offer you experience, different perspectives and their unique skillsets.

Sounds like a win-win to me.

Build For The Future – Training And Development

You may well have heard the phrase 'lifelong learning'. I firmly believe that continuous learning is important for everyone, and especially for inclusive workplace cultures. It's about setting yourself and others up for success. It's about being open to new ideas and perspectives.

But learning isn't always about attending formal training courses – we learn so much through experiential activities; by watching and listening to others. Whether we care to admit it or not, we are influenced by those we spend a lot of time with, which is why it's important to surround yourself with individuals that role model great behaviour. Also, be aware of the impact you have on others.

Set up for success

Everyone who chooses to be a manager or leader has a special obligation to be aware of the influence they have on people and situations. Employees look at the behaviour and actions of their managers and senior teams to see how they operate, and then follow their lead.

In my experience, when individuals are promoted into people management positions, they have to have what I call a 'magic weekend'. If they're promoted on a Friday, by the following Monday they're expected to have galvanised their people management experience and qualifications over the weekend and step confidently into the role of 'People Manager'. This is hardly fair to the individual or those they now must manage.

You need to set your managers up for success, particularly if you want to bring about a cultural change and create an inclusive workplace environment. Equip your managers with the right skills and tools to be strong and proficient, but not after they've been promoted. Prepare them and upskill their capability *before* they are promoted.

When it comes to policies and procedures, all managers need to be fully trained. This includes new manages as well as those who are more experienced. In the 'Take Stock' section of this book, I highlighted the importance of your company policies and procedures when you're creating an inclusive culture. These policies can and should change and evolve, so it's important that your managers are fully equipped with knowledge of policies so that they can use them to support employees swiftly and consistently. This is likely to include such things as recruitment, so managers must understand the roles they play in hiring decisions, how to manage the performance of team members, and how to support the health and wellbeing of team members through policies.

Leadership education

Leadership education needs to be aligned with the strategic direction of the organisation. If you know where your organisation is heading, ensure you develop your talent pool inclusively and have people with the right skills and capability in place to drive the business forward. Leadership education, therefore, needs to be inclusive. Make sure that it's not just certain individuals who are selected for management positions and offered training courses. Be open and transparent with training opportunities – they should be accessible to all, so consider the needs of underrepresented groups.

Also consider when and where training courses take place, making them accessible for all to attend. Take into account different learning styles and needs, and offer blended learning solutions.

Leadership education should be proactive. Don't just train somebody reactively when you've identified a gap within their capability. In a way, leadership education is an ongoing organic process that complements your talent attraction and retention strategy.

I would also encourage you to broaden your view of leadership learning. As we progress through life, we gain so much valuable experience. We don't gather much of this experience in the workplace, but it's incredibly transferrable.

For example, someone may say, 'I'm not very good at financial planning or accounting', yet they manage to run their homes and personal finances. Someone may say, 'I can't be a mentor', yet they help run a weekly local community group. Someone may say, 'I can't manage a project', yet every year they'll book a holiday or host a party or family event successfully. All this experience is transferrable into your working environment, so expand your view of learning and encourage your people to appreciate the value of 'life's learning' which is highly transferable to the workplace.

Women don't need fixing

I've acknowledged that my book does have a bias towards advancing women and increasing their presence within leadership positions. However, I'm a firm advocate for inclusivity across all underrepresented groups. Leadership education does need to be inclusive, so one way in which your organisation can support women or other underrepresented groups further is to run dedicated programmes. However, these should be part of a wider and more holistic programme and not stand alone.

For example, many companies now offer female leadership development programmes. There are some women, particularly aspiring leaders, who need additional support to enable them to build their confidence, share their thoughts and ideas, and find their voice. I deliver a women's leadership programme – JEWEL (Jungle Empowering Women to Excel at Leadership), but at this point I need to be really clear...

This programme isn't about fixing women.

Women don't need fixing!

Female leadership development programmes are about providing women with a learning environment that is relevant, inclusive and challenging, and equips them with the confidence to step into their brilliance. The important thing is to offer any such programme as part of your holistic approach to inclusion. For example, organisation structures need to be able to support the requirements of modern-day families, and women and other underrepresented groups need to be supported whether this be through development programmes and/or mentoring.

I also emphasise the importance of male advocates and ambassadors within the women leadership programmes my business delivers. As part of any female-orientated learning, women need to understand how to interact with their male counterparts and vice versa.

You may have heard of the book *Men Are from Mars, Women Are from Venus*. In short, the book highlights that males and females are essentially wired differently. By running development programmes aimed at supporting both groups, you can learn to recognise their natural differences and complementary talents, and find ways for them to communicate and work together.

Unconscious bias training

Helping managers and leaders realise that we all have our unique differences and there's a wealth of experience and talent around them every day is important. However, there is a danger that views can be skewed because of unconscious bias.

Training can raise awareness of how unconscious bias creeps into our conversations, the decisions we make and the behaviours we display, and highlight to people the consequences of their actions. However, as I pointed out in the 'Raise Awareness' section, research is showing that standalone unconscious bias training doesn't work. I've heard stories of companies running 'bitesize lunch and learn' unconscious bias training lasting no more than one hour. I've heard of companies offering e-learning modules which take about ten to fifteen minutes to complete. Such initiatives are superficial and can only skim over issues that are hidden and satisfy a tick-box exercise.

Your managers and leaders are never going to be magically transformed by sheep dipping them through training. Standalone unconscious bias training can cause more damage than good if it's not part of a holistic approach to your inclusion and diversity strategy, where you have a defined purpose. The outcome of a holistic and integrated approach, on the other hand, is powerful and transformative.

CASE STUDY – KEEPING IN TOUCH

I can give a personal example here of when leadership training wasn't inclusive and the impact an unconscious bias had on me.

Prior to going on maternity leave, I had an opportunity, with my fellow (I use the word 'fellow' because they were all male) leadership colleagues, to be sponsored by the company to move into the next phase of a qualification. The trouble was, this training course coincided with a period of time when I would have been on maternity leave.

I requested to use some of my 'keeping in touch' days (an initiative introduced by the UK government to enable women on maternity leave to stay connected with the business without it affecting their right to be on maternity leave) to attend the training course. It felt like a win-win situation to me. I was showing clear intent that I wanted to return, and be up to speed when I did so.

My request was denied.

I believe this decision was made as a result of unconscious bias. Because I wasn't going to be in the business for a period of time, I had become invisible. But I had a true desire to further my learning to enable me to operate on a level playing field with my colleagues upon my return.

In truth, my story is probably quite common. There will be many similar examples of people returning from periods of time away from the business, and decisions made through the lens of an unconscious bias can have impactful consequences. They can set people back, make them feel out of the loop, and increase the pressure in the work environment when they do return.

I urge you to raise awareness of the impact of unconscious bias within your organisation, but do so holistically and ensure that you follow through with support.

Apprenticeships and graduate programmes

As well as developing your existing talent, ensure that you are building talent for the future. Many organisations that want to become employers of choice work with local colleges and universities at an early stage, offering apprenticeship schemes and graduate programmes. This is a great way to build your talent pool.

Colleges and universities are only too keen to work with businesses to ensure that they are offering the right courses and skills, so I encourage you to reach out to further education providers and forge strong relationships. Companies that are proactive can get a competitive edge by aligning their learning programmes with a local education provider. It can also open up opportunities for existing employees of whatever age to gain external qualifications and improve their skills.

Apprenticeship schemes are great opportunities for individuals, whatever their age, gender, faith, race or background, to gain invaluable practical experience on the job. Graduate schemes are still offered by many companies and securing a place is highly competitive. If you offer a graduate scheme, consider how you will make your selection. Broaden the scope of where you select your graduates from. Look beyond attendance at educational establishments and consider the talent available from other socio-economic backgrounds.

Build for the future – Training and development summary

If you want your organisation to become inclusive, ensure that your selection processes for any training scheme are equitable and fair. Don't fall into the trap of unconscious bias and only select one type of person for a scheme.

Build For The Future – Summary And Checklist

In this section, we focused on the importance of building for the future. This will enable your organisation to shift its culture, align with your business strategy, and attract and retain talent from the widest pools.

Let's recap on some of the areas we've covered.

– **Business continuity**

☐ Do you have a business continuity and disaster recovery plan that includes your people?

☐ Are you able to effectively manage skill shortages, high staff turnover and loss of key staff members?

☐ Do you consider the travel planning arrangements when sending your key members of staff to annual conferences or events?

☐ Does your reward strategy align with your business continuity and talent plan?

☐ Have you considered alternative approaches to managing any staff skills shortages or ramping up your business workforce in order to meet customer demands?

– **Diversity and inclusion networks**

☐ Do you have a diversity and inclusion forum group in place?

☐ Does it span a number of underrepresented groups?

☐ Does it include representation by a senior leader/your diversity champion?

☐ Have you defined the purpose of the group to ensure it's focused on sharing experiences, educating others and suggesting practical measures to enhance diversity within your organisation, as opposed to being a place for militants to hang out?

☐ Does your diversity group enable individuals to feel proactively listened to and reassured that their suggestions are taken seriously and acted upon?

☐ Do you have representatives that participate in diversity and inclusion network groups outside of your organisation?

☐ Do you share the learnings from your own organisation with others?

☐ Do you invite other individuals into your organisation to share your experiences with them?

☐ Do you celebrate the successes or stories from the inclusion network groups that you either attend or host?

– **Talent planning**

☐ Do you have a formal process in place for talent planning?

☐ Do your managers understand their role in spotting talent?

☐ Do your managers understand their role in nurturing and developing talent within the organisation?

☐ Is your talent plan aligned with your business strategy?

☐ Have you created a talent map which details the skills and experience already available within your organisation?

☐ Do you keep your talent map and plan up to date?

☐ Do you calibrate your talent plan and map across a number of stakeholders to ensure the widest possible views, reducing unconscious bias?

☐ Do you link your talent plan with stretch opportunities?

☐ Do you ensure that your talent plan doesn't pigeonhole employees?

– **Returnships**

☐ Do you have a returnship/come back to work programme within your organisation?

☐ Is it open to all employees or is it set up for a specific group of individuals, eg women returning to work after maternity leave?

☐ Do you align your return to work programme with your leave/exit strategy so that you can track individuals and keep in touch with them?

☐ Do you ensure that there's a role available at the end of any returnship programme you offer?

☐ If you don't have the capacity to offer everyone who attends a returnship programme a role, do you partner with other organisations, inviting them to be aware of the talent you have developed?

☐ Have you reviewed your job descriptions to support return to work programmes?

☐ Do you have an on-boarding process, enabling those who participate in return to work schemes to be orientated into a team smoothly and quickly?

☐ Do you offer additional activities such as spending time in other departments?

☐ Do you have an open mind when selecting your returnship candidates, making sure they're not from the same moulds as your existing employees and being open to broad experiences?

☐ Do you get feedback from those participating in the programme, asking if the level of support they received was sufficient and whether you could make the programme even more successful?

Having the right talent in the right roles will enable your business to thrive. Putting systems and procedures in place to create an inclusive culture will ensure your people feel a sense of belonging when they come to work in an environment where they are respected and valued for their unique differences.

SECTION 5
EMBED

Embed – Introduction

Congratulations on getting this far in your inclusion journey! I'm sure that by now, you're well on your way to creating an inclusive workplace culture as the tribe5 Diversity & Inclusion methodology gives you a framework to follow. Hopefully you'll have implemented lots of new initiatives within your business or gained reassurance that you're heading in the right direction.

Embed is the final part of the tribe5 Diversity & Inclusion methodology, but it can often be the most difficult. Having a great inclusion plan is nothing without implementation. But I'm not talking about superficial implementation – I'm sure you know the sort. Everyone half-heartedly participates in a project in the hope that a new initiative will come along and they can heave a huge sigh of relief when things revert back to the 'good old days'. No, I'm talking about firmly embedding inclusion into your organisation so that no matter who is at the helm or what new initiatives you introduce, inclusion and diversity remain tightly woven into its fabric. It's at the heart of your organisation; it's your only way of being; it's your business as usual.

In the Embed section, we explore:

- The importance of **resilience** as you move along the inclusion journey

- How a **zero-tolerance** approach is not a get-out clause, but an opportunity for everyone to know what is acceptable

- How change can be accelerated through setting inclusion and **diversity goals** and milestones for everyone

- Why it's important to **monitor progress** – to check what's working and change what isn't

- To **celebrate success** along the way

So, let's get started.

Embed – Resilience And Zero Tolerance

Bringing about any change, including a cultural change (which is what you might require to create an inclusive culture), isn't going to happen overnight. It can take years to unpick ingrained behaviours and change hearts and minds, so resilience is going to be imperative.

Resilience is about making it stick. This requires focus, belief and determination.

Your organisation is likely to face many obstacles as you move towards a more inclusive and diverse culture. Barriers which you may need to overcome include:

- **Organisation structures** – an operating structure which is not fit for purpose and doesn't enable you to be agile and inclusive

- **Mindsets** – closed to differences and other perspectives

- **A lack of belief** – not fully accepting or having the confidence to believe that inclusion is important and will make a difference

- **Confidence** – women or minority groups lacking the confidence to put themselves forward, combined with a lack of support to enable them to do so

- **Working patterns** – preferring presenteeism to engagement and productivity, meaning you're unable to focus on the business reasons for using flexible working

- **Technology** – employees are closed to advancements and embracing a better way of delivering solutions

- **Workforce demographics** – a failure to understand the workforce and respond to the needs of different generations

- **Policies and procedures** – these may act as barriers rather than enablers for growth

- **Lack of talent** – you have a significant skills gap as you are unable to attract and retain talent

In truth, there are likely to be other barriers that you have to overcome, some that you don't even know about yet. I recognise that the journey will be difficult and long, so to help you deal with the bumps in the road, here are some top tips.

Be clear on what you're aiming for

Do you know what it'll feel like when you've achieved your vision? John Whitmore's GROW model is a great framework to use to explore this as it sets out clear steps to help you consider the point further:

- **G**oal – define and agree the goal or outcome you want to achieve

- **R**eality – what are you currently doing?

- **O**ptions – what could you do to achieve the goal/outcome?

- **W**ay forward – what do you have the will to do?

The GROW model can be used as part of your own thinking around inclusion, or with teams to aid alignment.

Are the challenges real or perceived?

Sometimes restrictions are not real; they are in fact born of our own perceptions of the challenge, so we place restrictions upon ourselves or others.

I hear people say, 'We're not allowed', or 'We can't', but the reality can be different when I explore further. Often no-one has actually said, 'You're not allowed' or 'You can't'; it's other factors which have prevented something from happening, so it's worth exploring if the resistance which you have to overcome is real, or if it's perceived based upon stories and traditions.

Stand firm in your convictions

You'll need to be firm about your convictions and dedicated to achieving the outcomes. To do this may require a degree of strength and mental toughness.

In their book, *Developing Mental Toughness: Gold Medal Strategies for Transforming your Business Performance* (Sept 2008) Professor Graham Jones and Adrian Moorhouse MBE identify four pillars that form the foundation of sustained high performance:

- Maintain emotional stability when you're under stress
- Believe in yourself

– Find your source of motivation so you can keep going

Don't lose sight of what matters. These four attitudes have been specifically identified in studies of elite performers, although it's important to highlight that mental toughness isn't the same as being physically and mentally hard, ruthless or stubborn. It's not about suppressing emotions and pushing yourself to extreme limits when it is not sensible to do so. Mental toughness is a trait and characteristic of an inclusive leader – an individual who is open, fair-minded, caring and decent, good at controlling their thoughts and acting rationally and constructively when the pressure is on.[27]

Review, refresh and reinforce

One of the reasons why I developed tribe5 Diversity & Inclusion as a cyclical methodology is because the process doesn't end. You'll have to continually go back and review. Revisit your data – take stock of what is working and identify things that haven't landed quite as well as you'd hoped.

It's all about asking 'Well, what did work?' and 'What can we do differently next time?' Measure and celebrate the successes that you've had. Use these

---

27 *Developing Mental Toughness* – Prof Graham Jones and Adrian Moorhouse MBE

triumphs to reinforce your aim and keep the momentum building – remember that there's likely to be an ebb and flow of people in your organisation, so keep your vision fresh and alive. Communicate with clarity and consistency, enabling your inclusive culture to continue to develop and grow.

Zero tolerance

Zero tolerance is holding people to account, addressing behaviour and conduct infringements. To achieve zero tolerance, everyone must have absolute clarity on the aim of the organisation. They must understand the rules and know what is required of them to enable them to abide by the rules.

Your company policies and procedures will provide clarity around operating practices. Your leaders and managers will set the tone of your organisation, so you need to check their behaviour is congruent. As the saying goes, 'Do the words and the music go together?' Until your desired culture becomes ingrained, there may be times when company employees at all levels are tempted to slip back into old ways of thinking. That's when it's important to stand firm and, if necessary, show zero tolerance.

Embed – Resilience and zero tolerance summary

You will have challenges to overcome while embedding an inclusive and diverse culture in your organisation, and at times the process may be glacial, so you will need resilience to ensure that you keep moving forward. You'll also need to be agile, particularly as you flex with the economic landscape as it unfolds. Remember, inclusion isn't about taking things away – it's about adding more to the mix.

Embed – Creating A Plan

It's great to have lots of ideas about initiatives which you could, should or must do, but quite frankly, nothing's going to happen unless you take action. Equally, taking action without a plan won't get you very far.

Kindle desires

One of my absolute favourite business books is *Will It Make the Boat Go Faster?* by Ben Hunt-Davies and Harriet Beveridge. If you've not read this book, then I highly recommend it (after you've finished this one, of course).

The book reflects upon Ben's Olympic gold medal-winning journey. For Ben and his fellow rowers, team work and goal setting were key components of their success, enabling them to cross the finish line in first place at the Sydney 2000 Olympics and achieve their collective goal of becoming gold medallists.

One of the ways in which Ben and his crew achieved their victory was through the formulation of layered goals. Each layer elicited a feeling, behaviour or action and formed the stepping stones to success:

- The crazy layer – Impassioned feelings
- The concrete layer – Determinable outcomes
- The control layer – Pragmatic
- The everyday layer – Actionable[28]

My challenge to you is to make your inclusion goal extravagant. Make it bold and inspiring – so much so that it ignites energy and passion within others. By creating an inclusion goal which sparks an emotional attachment, you will compel your workforce will feel drawn towards achieving it.

---

28 *Will It Make the Boat Go Faster?* Ben Hunt-Davis and Harriet Beveridge

The power of three

Once you've defined your goal, it's important to commit to three key objectives that you intend to focus on and against which you will measure progress. Too many objectives can make the end goal feel overwhelming and potentially unachievable. Too few may mean that you're unlikely to make sufficient progress towards achieving your end goal, so three is an ideal number. The next step is to turn your overall goal and your three key focus areas/objectives into a plan.

I love a good plan! In fact, I've often worked with boards to create plans. We go off-site for a couple of days. At the end of this time, the team has formulated a strategic plan. Brilliant.

However, what often happens is the team goes back to the office and gets bogged down in the day-to-day business operation. When the time comes to review the strategic plan, they report little or no progress. Your inclusion and diversity plan doesn't need to be complex, but it does need to be a living, workable plan, not a document that sits in a drawer somewhere and is dusted down occasionally. Yes, of course it needs to be documented, but everyone in your organisation absolutely needs to live and breathe the plan every day. So your inclusion and diversity plan needs to align with, support and complement the overall strategic direction of the organisation.

Establish if there are any other change initiatives taking place within your organisation which could derail the achievement of your goal. Or could they be complementary? These initiatives could include the implementation of a new IT system or the change of a working process, both of which create an opportunity for change to occur. This change won't come about as a direct consequence of diversity, but you can ensure that diversity and inclusion are woven into all initiatives.

Get everyone involved

Share your goal widely with everyone. Set inclusion objectives for employees at all levels. Monitor progress towards the attainment of the key areas/objectives you have set out by regularly reporting at board level and in one-to-one conversations with line managers.

 If you're not sure how every employee can get involved, you could include activities such as:

- Getting to know colleagues in a different department

- Sitting next to someone different and talking to them during lunch once a week

- Having an email-free day so you must go and find people to talk to them

- Taking turns to chair weekly meetings

- Setting up or attending network groups for underrepresented individuals

- Hosting or giving talks on inclusion and diversity, or sharing the best practice you operate within your organisation

- Identifying stretch opportunities for individuals

- Redefining job roles

These are just a few examples; you'll need to create ones relevant for your organisation. Whatever activities you embark upon, make sure they lead towards the achievement of the central goal.

Your inclusion guiding team

Create an inclusion guiding team. Often these include members of your leadership team who will also act as champions; the bold voices, the advocates. Your inclusion guiding team will hold each other and the organisation accountable, so when progress isn't happening or when you slip back into old ways, the team will call it out. Equally, when your organisation is making progress, the team will ensure that success is celebrated.

Embed – Creating a plan summary

Success will come through making sure that whatever actions you and your employees take every day, they are moving you towards your inclusion goal. I'd love to learn that you have not only delivered against your inclusion and diversity plan as a consequence of reading this book, but you've transformed your organisational culture and are winning awards as a result.

Now that's a bold and extravagant goal!

Embed – Forums And Networks

Employee forums and networks can have a positive impact on an organisation. You may already have some forums/networks in place, such as health and safety, Great Place to Work, or wellbeing groups. These groups may meet on a regular basis, sharing their experiences of the organisation with a view to assisting the company to enhance the working environment.

Inclusion and diversity networks and forums can add tremendous value to your organisation. They are a great opportunity for underrepresented groups to come together to share experiences, meet new individuals, and potentially educate others to gain fresh perspectives. But these groups absolutely are not places for militants to hang out and moan. Therefore, it's important when you're setting up such groups to define their purpose, which should be to focus on sharing experiences, educating others and suggesting practical measures to enhance inclusion and diversity within your organisation.

Hearing first hand

Networks and forums offer a range of benefits to both the employer and employee. They're opportunities for you to hear directly from diverse employees about their views and experiences of working within your organisation, so make sure members of your leadership attend these groups – it's a great opportunity for them to listen, engage in open dialogue and act.

In the *Inspire and Involve* section, I covered the importance of accessible role models. You can invite these individuals to attend and be guest speakers at any inclusion and diversity networking forum events that you organise. On the whole, role models will be individuals from within your organisation, but they may also come in as a result of you developing relationships with the local communities. By seeking out external opportunities as well as developing internal networks, you will open the opportunities for wider conversations to take place in relation to diversity and inclusion, expanding relationships and sharing best practice knowledge and initiatives.

You may be fortunate within your own organisation to have large support teams coupled with the financial budget to progress your inclusion journey more swiftly. Conversely, you may just be starting out on your journey and have limited knowledge and resources. Through collaboration and the sharing of your inclusion and diversity activities at networking groups, you will give everyone the opportunity to make progress more quickly, strengthening your brand reputation in the process.

It's not too late

If you have not already done so, I would highly encourage you to participate in or set up your own inclusion and diversity network(s). It may be necessary to set up multiple networks to cover a range of underrepresented groups so that you can open more dialogue, or you may just wish to set up one in the first instance. Whichever option you choose, the essence of these groups is inclusivity, so make them accessible to all employees. Consider practical things such as when and where these groups take place. Make sure there's the ability for individuals to access them and participate remotely.

Embed – Forums and networks summary

Diversity and inclusion networks will create great opportunities for your business and individuals. They're wonderful ways to open dialogue and keep the conversations going, providing opportunities to connect, share experiences, educate others and gain fresh perspectives. These networks can really help to reinforce and embed inclusion and diversity in your organisation.

Embed – The Role Of Communication

One of the most difficult challenges for any organisation today is to find ways to speak to its employees effectively. Communicating with employees regularly ensures everyone understands the business objectives and goals, as well as their place in achieving these as part of an inclusive culture, but with ever-changing technology offering new ways to communicate, businesses must ensure that they're reaching their people in a way that suits them.

While a printed memo might have done the trick a few decades ago, or a 'copy all' email more recently, organisations must now tackle the challenges of communicating to many generations of employees. Some employees, especially the younger generations, will expect the instant, fun and globally-accessible aspects of the social media they enjoy in their personal lives to carry over to their professional lives.

Effective communication sits at the heart of employee engagement. Let's face it, it's hard to find arguments against having an engaged workforce, particularly if you're creating an inclusive workplace culture. I shared with you in the '*Raise Awareness – Employee Engagement And Recognition*' chapter that engaged employees are more loyal, productive and committed to the organisation they work for. They tend to go above and beyond the call of duty, putting in discretionary effort. Engaged employees also provide more innovative ideas because they truly want the business to succeed, so they look for opportunities to suggest improvements.

Effective communication is central to this level of employee engagement.

The recipe for success

 A communication strategy will set the tone for the organisation's message as well as the delivery method, helping people become increasingly engaged. Effective communication is like a recipe, and every communication strategy will require a different mix of ingredients because every organisation's culture is different. But, like in many dishes, there's some ingredients that need to be in the mix every time. The ingredients listed below will need to be in the mix every time:

- A clear, consistent message with the appropriate level of information
- Openness and honesty with an authentic tone
- Passion and connection
- Goals, purpose and direction
- Clarity, transparency, measurement and accountability

These ingredients may seem straightforward and obvious, but far too often organisations get so focused on the business side of things, they forget the regular human connection they require for employees to be truly engaged. Review your recent communications and see if they include all the ingredients – it's a hard recipe to create initially, but it gets easier once everyone is in the habit of communicating in an open and authentic way.

Communicating to a collective of unique individuals

Every person will have their own way of communicating, and we all have a way in which we prefer others to communicate with us. We are similar, yet we are different. Everyone is unique, so what you need to engage your employees as a collective group can sometimes be hard to find, let alone get right. Some will not respond well to written communication. Others will switch off when senior management are speaking. A few will respond to visual communication such as images, graphs, diagrams and employee engagement noticeboards. If you really want to engage with everyone, you need to create spoken, visual and written communications (including your website and social media platforms) which set out what an inclusive culture looks and feels like.

The tone of voice you use is important. The language you will use to communicate with senior management will be different from the language you use when talking to generation Z, graduates or trainees. But you want all your workforce to understand and trust what you are saying.

Keep communication simple and consistent and be human – don't be too formal. Avoid jargon or acronyms if you want wider understanding. You should also check what you say for any unconscious bias and ensure you are being fair and inclusive to all protected characteristics. There are apps and web-based tools such as Textio and Gender Decoder that can help strip out words that might appeal less to women than men.

Listen

Remember that communication involves listening, too. It's no good just talking at staff. From daily feedback between managers and staff to team meetings, regular surveys, suggestion schemes or employee-led groups, there are many ways to listen to employees' recommendations.

Make listening and responding to employee feedback a part of your overall internal communication process. Employees want to feel that they have been heard. It's also important to keep them apprised of any progress.

The role of leaders

How can your organisation ensure that the messages you want to get across are communicated effectively and work towards improving employee engagement? Fostering a culture that is open and honest among all team members has a tremendous impact on engagement and business outcomes, so it's critical that your leaders and managers are all on board with your engagement approach.

When line managers and employees communicate effectively, it enables everyone to have clarity around what is being asked of them. It also allows for greater understanding of the role people play, and can aid personal development as employees may be encouraged to take part in new initiatives.

 Effective communication can include:

One-to-one time – where discussions are open. This means sometimes getting off track and talking about non-critical business issues – and that's OK. It's during those moments that relationships are built and strengthened, and some of the most creative ideas can be sparked. These discussions are made more difficult when people are working remotely or when everyone just seems 'too busy' to have a chat. Encourage managers to talk to their staff and ask them how their day is going.

Use technology to your advantage. Consider an intranet site where people can post pictures and status updates, and comment on each other's posts. Creating a (moderated) intranet platform that mirrors social media sites like Facebook opens the floodgates to communication in a way that people are used to in their personal lives.

Film clips – use smart devices to record short film clips of senior leaders talking on business updates, sharing progress on projects, or reinforcing key messages such as the importance of your inclusion journey. Video clips are a great way of enabling employees to put a face to a name while allowing leaders to show they are authentic and aligned with the message.

Podcasts – create podcasts on important topics. Interview staff members and ask them to be involved. These are great for sharing experiences and educating others.

Giving feedback – when you're giving feedback to an employee, be mindful about not only when and how you deliver this, but also the choice of language you use. I've often heard phraseology such as, 'Man-up and deal with it', so tune in to what you're saying. Think about the language you want to encourage and the language you want to stamp out.

Storytelling – gather stories that play back the past, remind people about the present, and create excitement about the future and the role they play in its creation. What stories are currently being shared within your business? Storytelling is hugely important because you can really bring in the listener. Individuals often align themselves with stories, so use them to celebrate successes and inspire others.

Sofa sessions and 'KitKat breaks' – these are informal sessions which employees share with members of the leadership team, providing employees with a safe environment to ask any questions on their mind in a small group without fear or embarrassment. The relaxed environment is a great place to open dialogue around particular topics. You could set 'topics of the month' that you want to hear about and invite everyone to prepare questions in advance.

Values-based themed weeks – these activities can promote working together to embed the company values. They could include a creativity week when you celebrate an innovative idea an employee put forward that has gone on to make a different to others. It could be a 'dare to aspire' week when guest speakers come in to share their career journeys, or business leaders go out into local communities to share their journeys with schools and colleges to inspire the future generations.

Leadership walkabouts – park your car in a different car park or take a different route to get to your office. By doing this, you will meet new people. The key is to stop and strike up a conversation. Enquire about your people's day – get to know them.

Leadership lunches – similar to the sofa sessions, these are a great way for the leadership team to meet different employees.

Team briefings – introduce a cascade approach to team briefings. Include a written script with key points which is cascaded to all employees. Each manager could swap departments and brief a different team. This helps managers to meet teams from across the organisation, it breaks down silos and builds relationships.

Resource materials – make sure company communication materials, such as briefing documents, posters, factsheets, are engaging and informative. They often share important business information, so make them short, jargon free, punchy and easy to read. They should also signpost your employees where to go if they want more information.

Recognition schemes – you could introduce engagement schemes such as the SHINE awards I detailed in the *'Raise Awareness – Employee Engagement And Recognition'* chapter. Every month or quarter, employees can be recognised for the great work they are doing. There are doubtless lots of things going on within your organisation that can and should be celebrated.

These simple things can go a long way towards enhancing engagement, which will in turn translate into better productivity and increased efficiency and cohesiveness. Most organisations rely on team spirit and camaraderie to make the business operate in a cohesive fashion.

Keep employees in the loop

Employees who are part of an inclusive and diverse culture want to know where the organisation is going and how they contribute. One of the best ways to keep the organisation heading towards its goals is to increase the level of communication between senior leaders and employees.

Take gender pay reporting, for example. Organisations in the UK that have over 250 employees now have to report this information on an annual basis. The requirement is for these companies to submit the data to the UK government's website and display it on their company intranet. While it's not compulsory, organisations are also encouraged to provide narrative on how they intend to close the gap.

This is a golden opportunity and not something to shy away from. Create a narrative that acknowledges your current position while setting out the things you are committed to focusing on. As well as publishing this externally, I would encourage you to weave it into your wider internal communication plan so that every employee understands where you are now and what you are doing about it.

You can also share this information with customers and stakeholders as it highlights your plans to close the gap through increasing your inclusion initiatives, showcasing your level of commitment towards creating an inclusive culture to prospective as well as current employees.

Embed – The role of communication summary

Everyone wants to feel that they matter. When employees recognise that their opinions make a difference, they are more likely to actively engage in the organisation's culture.

You need to encourage your employees to be vocal. Give them lots of different routes to make their voices heard and let them know that you will listen to any feedback, acting on it where necessary. Ensure that you have open and honest discussions with no subject being off limits.

Communication is the cornerstone of an engaged workforce. Implementing some of the best practices I have outlined in this chapter will help you to connect with your employees and move towards an engaged, diverse and inclusive workforce, contributing to the most successful business outcomes.

Embed – Celebrating Success

I know that bringing about a culture change – which is essentially what you are doing as you are creating your inclusive workplace culture – won't be easy. It's going to be a long and possibly difficult journey, which is why it's essential to celebrate all the successes you have along the way.

Celebrate and shout about all the small wins. Athletes know only too well that it's these marginal gains that make a difference and keep people engaged, but sometimes in business, we can be so focused on the end destination, we forget to enjoy the journey along the way.

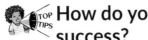 **How do you identify and share success?**

- Make sure you have your base data so that you know what success looks like, otherwise how will you know when you have reached a point where you can celebrate success?

- What gets measured gets done, so you need to make all members of your leadership team responsible for improvements in diversity and inclusion, and for highlighting wins that can be celebrated.

- Celebrating and sharing all your employees' successes is important. Don't just do it in a brief way; to really embed any learning in the culture, you need to talk about the impact that a success has had, no matter how small. Create case studies and tell a story. Talk about the why and the how and the people behind the success.

- Think about the actions you may have taken to improve diversity and inclusion in your organisation, from implementing programmes to new ways of working, processes and ideas. I have spoken about many of these throughout this book.

- If you have made improvements to your gender pay gap, publicise your report on your internet and social media presence, newsletters and with staff.

- Have you appointed male ambassadors? Who are they, what is their role, why did they volunteer, and what progress have they made?

- How many women have gone through your leadership development programme? What did they learn? Where are they now? How are they making a difference? What are their plans?

- Have you set up an employee-led group that is discussing diversity issues? What suggestions have they made that have been implemented and what is the impact?

- Have you won any awards or received external recognition for your people, diversity or inclusion strategies?

These are just a few things you can do to celebrate. The important thing is to recognise the progress which you and your employees are making as it gives you all renewed energy to keep going.

Sharing success internally

It's all too easy for senior management and board members to take the credit for the accolades that come with success. But any great leader will want to share the success, earning the respect of their teams and employees.

By empowering and motivating your team, you will improve both an individual's and an organisation's performance, staff loyalty and discretionary effort. It's important to understand that your staff are likely to respond in different ways when they are involved in a successful project. I'm a Licensed Practitioner of the personality profiling tool Insights Discovery, which can help increase personal awareness, improve team effectiveness, strengthen internal and external relationships and improve communication.

Let's use the Insights Discovery model to identify the four personality types and how they react.

Fiery red will be focused on task and action and be keen to move on to the next thing. A leader with a fiery red personality will need to pause, acknowledging that the project was successful, allowing others to celebrate and rejuvenate before rushing on to the next one.

Sunshine yellow will want to shout from the rooftops about the success. Harness this enthusiasm and involve them in the celebration process. Get them to write up their experiences and stories so that they can be shaped into internal and external communications later.

Earth green will want to celebrate collectively, valuing the enhanced team spirit. Encourage this, ensuring that opportunities are available for teams to get together to celebrate their success.

Cool blue will value the measurability of the change. Cool blue leaders have a gift for thinking analytically. Make them responsible for creating the base data and surveying or measuring the change so you can learn from the experience and make improvements.

Further details on the Insights Discovery tool can be found on my website https://www.junglehr.com/bespoke_programmes_training/insights-discovery/

Sharing with others

It is important to share your best practice learning with others, both inside and outside your organisation. It will help to accelerate your employees' inclusion journey while enhancing your company brand.

Large organisations can team up with smaller organisations or non-commercial bodies like charities or colleges to share success stories. These are more tangible than strategies, plans and statistics, so make your stories about your people.

I'd love to hear about your success stories – so do get in touch and email me atTribe5@junglediversity.com. By sharing your stories, you are further embedding your learning. I want to hear you say, 'It's worked!' and 'This is how we did it, and this is the impact it is having'.

Embed – Celebrating success summary

You may feel that your organisation's success comes about because you have the best product or service. But the truth is if you don't have the right people in your organisation, success is never going to happen.

Sharing success helps you to recognise the people behind the wins and tell the world how proud you are of them. And in return, your people will say how proud they are of your progress on your diversity and inclusion journey.

Embed – Summary And Checklist

One of the reasons why I developed tribe5 Diversity & Inclusion as a cyclical methodology is because the process doesn't end. You continually need to go back and review your progress to make sure inclusion and diversity are embedded firmly in your organisation's culture. No matter who is at the helm, inclusion and diversity must remain at the heart of your business. This can take a lot of hard work, often changing behaviours and mindsets in the process, but it is so worth it.

Let's recap what we have learned in this section.

Embed checklist

– **Resilience and zero tolerance**

☐ Is your operating structure fit for purpose? Does it enable you to be agile and inclusive?

☐ Are mindsets within your organisation open to differences and other perspectives?

☐ Does everyone within your organisation truly believe inclusion is important and will make a difference?

☐ Do women or other minority groups have the confidence to put themselves forward?

☐ Do they have the right level of support to enable them to do so?

☐ Do you offer flexible working, or do you favour presenteeism over engagement and productivity?

☐ Is your organisation open to advancements and embracing a better way of delivering solutions?

☐ Do you understand your workforce and respond to the needs of different generations?

☐ Do your policies and procedures act as enablers for growth?

☐ Are you able to attract and retain talent, or does your organisation suffer from significant skills gaps?

☐ Are the challenges you face real or perceived?

☐ Are you standing firm in your convictions?

☐ Do you demonstrate zero tolerance towards behaviour incongruent with an inclusive culture?

- **Creating a plan**

☐ Is your inclusion plan bold and inspiring?

☐ Do you have three key objectives that you intend to focus on, against which you will measure progress?

☐ Is your inclusion and diversity plan alive?

☐ Does it align with, support and complement the overall strategic direction of the organisation?

☐ Have you shared it widely across the organisation?

☐ Have you developed inclusion objectives for everyone at all levels?

☐ Have you created an inclusion guiding team?

- **Forums and networks**

☐ Have you created inclusion and diversity network and forum groups in your organisation?

☐ Do you ensure that members of your leadership team attend these groups?

☐ Are your inclusion and diversity networks accessible to everyone?

☐ Have you given consideration to when and where your networks and forums take place?

– **The role of communication**

☐ Does your communication strategy engage people?

☐ Does it have a clear, consistent message with the appropriate level of information?

☐ Is it open and honest with an authentic tone?

☐ Does it have passion and connection?

☐ Does it have goals, purpose and direction?

☐ Does it have clarity, transparency, measurement and accountability?

☐ Does it resonate with a diverse group of people?

☐ How do you ensure your message is communicated effectively?

☐ What is the role of your leaders and managers in communicating this message?

☐ How do you keep all employees in the loop?

- **Celebrating success**

  ☐ How do you identify and share success?

  ☐ Do you make sure everyone across the organisation is included in the celebration?

  ☐ How do you share your best practice learning with others?

Conclusion

That's it – technically you've done it all.

By now, you should have accessed all employee touchpoints within your business – which start before you've even attracted people through the door. You're likely to have taken proactive steps to weave diversity into the structure of your organisation, so that no matter who is at the helm, inclusiveness is part of your routine.

You'll have overcome some of the initial challenges, but there are likely to be more – so it's absolutely imperative that you keep going. Stay on the path of inclusion, celebrating successes along the way and continuing to remind everybody why it's important.

Evaluate what's working and identify what isn't, taking steps to tweak and change. Business is forever evolving, so your relationship with inclusion and diversity needs to evolve too. We will all have a different starting point. What works for one organisation may not be right for you. The important thing is to start (if you've not already done so).

Whichever area you choose to focus your attention on, stick to it and make it real. Create ways in which your people can see, feel and hear the difference your inclusive culture brings. Keep it alive. It's not a process that starts and has a definite ending, or just needs dusting down every year; it's something that carries on perpetually, so it will feel like a marathon, not a sprint.

And it's not easy – I know from personal experience how hard a marathon is. My sister and I completed a 26-mile moonlight walk in aid of Cancer Research in memory of our mum, who battled with cancer for over twenty-six years. Neither of us had trained properly (although I do walk my dogs). My sister was, in fact, advised not to complete the walk on medical grounds as she has had a double hip replacement. It was, however, important to both of us, and so we entered the charity walk and, on the night, went at a pace that was comfortable for us. We talked, walked, hobbled, laughed and cried along the way, but eventually we completed the walk and achieved our goal.

In a similar manner, your inclusion journey won't be easy at times. You'll have people telling you, 'It can't be done' and 'It won't work'. You'll have people who just won't understand why it's important to do it at all as 'We're OK as we are' and 'It's not broken, so nothing needs fixing'. You might make a quick start, but then need encouragement and support to keep going as faith or stamina waver along the way.

By setting out your clear intention, creating milestones and celebrating successes as you go along, you'll build momentum and achieve your aim. Great things can be achieved when you and your employees step forward together.

CASE STUDY – IS THAT ALL YOU'VE GOT?

James Taylor, former Sodexo Healthcare UK and Ireland CEO, shared this story at an Inclusive Companies event I attended. The event was the National Diversity Awards launch and was intended to highlight the importance of diversity and inclusion within the workplace.

James shared the work that Sodexo has been doing in this field. His presence was captivating, and his speech 'Rise Up' was so incredibly powerful and provocative – I loved it!

He said, 'It's really important to rise up, to stand on the shoulders of people who have gone before in order to make the difference and to push for change to happen. As part of that rising up, you have to reach down and bring people with you along the way.'

Right from his early childhood, through school, further education, in his professional career and even today, whenever James shares his achievements with his father, the older man listens and then says, 'Is that all you've got?'

This statement isn't intended to be negative; James's father recognises that if his son has achieved all of these great things, he's still got more within him to achieve.

I firmly believe that inclusion has to be inclusive. It has to involve everyone. Your organisation has a responsibility to provide the platform for everyone to 'rise up', but everyone needs to play their part. Your role is to enable others to stand on your shoulders, as you stood on the shoulders of those who went before you. But reach back and bring everyone with you. Help others to understand the role and contribution they play in creating a better workplace.

In the words of James Taylor, I challenge you, 'Is that all you've got?' If you think you've already created an inclusive workplace culture, is that all you've got? If you believe you've got a diverse workforce, is that all you've got? If you've made attempts to close the gap, is that all you've got? Quite frankly, I think you're capable of more.

Next steps – where to start

The first thing to do is congratulate yourself. In reading this book, you've given yourself a clearer idea of where you need to start, and if you've filled in the Diversity & Inclusion Scorecard too, then you'll have received additional recommendations to improve each of the TRIBE stages. To access the scorecard, please visit www.junglediversity. com/diconsultancy/tribe5-diversity-inclusion/ diversity-inclusion-scorecard/

You've come a long way in understanding where your organisation currently has gaps and acknowledging that you need to implement and effect necessary change. The temptation will be to try to do everything all at once. Don't! This can be an overwhelming a task, so don't run the risk of diluting your results in key areas that require the most immediate attention and where you will achieve the biggest impact on the business.

 Sign up to the TRIBE Charter as your primary tool and follow these top tips to move you forward:

- Identify three key areas that require immediate attention and where the impact of change will be the greatest

- Create an action plan. If you don't have one, you can download Jungle's 'Action Plan for Success' template from https://www.junglehr.com/ free-resources/

- Break the key areas down into small steps, enabling you to tackle targeted objectives and gain momentum as you implement your plan

- Communicate the plan widely and openly with all employees

- Offer everyone a role to play so they can hold each other to account

- Weave the objectives into the leadership agenda

- Measure and track progress

- Celebrate success along the way – remember it's the marginal gains that make a difference

- Evaluate the change

- Identify another key focus area and continue to build on the progress you've already made

These steps demonstrate your proactive commitment to bringing about a change of culture to create an organisation that is both inclusive and celebrates diversity. Not only does this send a positive message to your employees, it also signals to both clients and competitors that your business is committed to embracing diversity and inclusion as part of its standard policies and procedures.

Summary

The purpose of this book was to provide you with a framework to help you in your pursuit of an inclusive workplace culture.

Make/turn your organisation into the destination of choice for those who seek an inclusive environment. An environment filled with individuals from diverse backgrounds, preferences, sexual orientations and economic groups. My vision is for you to follow the tribe5 Diversity & Inclusion methodology. Through your commitment to hire, develop, reward and retain exceptional people, you will create the place where you can bring together the best of society.

Exceptional people come in all forms, shapes and sizes, and from all backgrounds. For me, the creation of the tribe5 Diversity & Inclusion methodology was personal. I've had social labels applied to me which have made my life and career journey unnecessarily challenging at times. I've experienced companies that have an inclusive environment at the heart of everything they do. Equally, I've experienced organisations that didn't value unique differences. Unless an employee fitted the mould, looking, speaking and behaving in a way that matched the organisations' ideal, then they didn't get on.

Our society has changed dramatically, and will continue to do so. And our places of work need to keep pace. So follow TRIBE and create an environment where employees with different backgrounds and perspectives can feel like they belong. Then both the organisation and its people can step into their brilliance and achieve their true potential.

Those companies just starting out in creating an inclusive workplace culture, I commend you. Those of you already well on the way to creating an inclusive workplace culture, I thank you, but I also challenge you as there's always more you can do. My call to action to you, and to everyone reading this book, is to make sure that you continue to reach out to new groups of people. Build relationships with colleges, universities, communities and professions. Those with different values and perspectives to the ones you currently have in your organisation.

I'm personally committed to enabling organisations to create an inclusive workplace culture where unconscious bias plays no part. Where everyone respects each other and values unique differences on the basis of merit. Above all, I want organisations to apply the tribe5 Diversity & Inclusion methodology and create environments where people feel they can be their best. Where they don't need to hide any part of who they are.

Through this book, I want to widen the inclusivity and diversity debate beyond that of gender. As we move forward and make progress, it's vital that we focus on other areas, such as black, Asian and minority ethnic (BAME) colleagues, sexuality and migrant workers, at the same time. Gender diversity certainly includes all these areas since 50% of the population is female. It shouldn't matter what your colour is, what sexuality you identify with or where you come from. Diversity and inclusion form the umbrella under which we *all* sit.

Not only is our society changing, but the workforce and its attitudes are also changing. A whole host of millennial workers, and their own children, expect to be treated differently to the way that workers have been treated historically. The time to act is now.

Follow the tribe5 Diversity & Inclusion methodology with a view to creating real and meaningful change within your business.

I hope this book has made you stop and think about the future – because if you are reporting on your workforce year on year, you need to know what you're going to say next year and in all the years to come. If your statistics are the same and you're essentially painting the same picture as before, or a worse picture, then you're in for a tough time. Equally, I hope I've helped raise your own awareness and that you'll use the tools I've suggested to implement and execute change. Finally, I hope I've inspired you to want to develop a business or a corporation that will be the envy of your competitors.

Acknowledgements

To my husband Mike, for supporting me unquestionably, for believing in me and enabling me to do what I love.

To my children Melanie and James, and my granddaughter Leigh, for the love we share and the treasured memories we create.

To my dear friend Tim, for his unrelenting support, for the honest yet kind feedback and for keeping me on course.

To Mike, Lucy, Joe and Verity at Rethink for your constructive challenge and faith in me, but above all for bringing my book to life.

To all my family, friends and colleagues who have offered encouragement, words of wisdom and wine when necessary!

To all my wonderful clients with whom I'm privileged to partner.

Finally, but certainly not least, to you for reading this book. My hope is that you can step into your brilliance.